Time Stood Still

Madeleine Hill.

Time Stood Still

Madeleine Hill

First published in Great Britain in 2003 by
SPCK
Holy Trinity Church
Marylebone Road
London NW1 4DU

British Library Cataloguing-in-Publication Data
A catalogue record for this book is available from the British Library

ISBN 0-281-05295-6

1 3 5 7 9 10 8 6 4 2

Typeset by Avocet Typeset, Chilton, Aylesbury, Bucks
Printed in Great Britain by Bookmarque Ltd, Croydon, Surrey

Contents

Acknowledgements

Unless otherwise stated, Scripture quotations are from the New Revised Standard Version of the Bible, copyright 1989 by the Division of Christian Education of the National Council of the Churches of Christ in the USA. Used by permission. All rights reserved.

Where no source is shown, extracts were related to the author personally.

Extracts from the following publications are reproduced by permission:

Sadhu Sundar Singh by C. F. Andrew. Reproduced by permission of Hodder and Stoughton Limited.

I Died Three Times in 1977 by P. M. H. Atwater. Used by permission of the author (http://www.cinemind.com/atwater).

The Hiding Place by Corrie ten Boom with John and Elizabeth Sherrill. Reproduced by permission of Hodder and Stoughton Limited and of Chosen Books LLC, Chappaqua, NY.

Saved! by Tony Bullimore, published by Little, Brown. Reproduced by permission of Time Warner Books UK.

Surprised by the Voice of God by Jack S. Deere. Copyright © 1996 by Jack S. Deere. Used by permission of Zondervan.

Secret Affairs of the Soul by Paul Hawker. Reproduced by permission of Northstone Publishing.

Exploring Inner Space by David Hay, published by Penguin. Reproduced by permission.

Religious Experience Today by David Hay, published by Mowbray (1990). Reproduced by permission of Continuum.

Seeing Angels by Emma Heathcote-James (Blake Publishing, 2001). Used by permission of Blake Publishing, 3 Bramber Court, 2 Bramber Road, London W14 9PB, tel: 020 7381 0666.

Memories, Dreams and Reflections by C. G. Jung, edited by

Acknowledgements

Aniela Jaffe, translated by Richard and Clara Winston, copyright © 1961, 1962, 1963 and renewed 1989, 1990, 1991 by Random House Inc. Used by permission of Pantheon Books, a division of Random House, Inc.

Christ With Us by Roy Lawrence. Reproduced by permission of the author.

Some Other Rainbow by John McCarthy and Jill Morrell published by Bantam Press. Used by permission of Transworld Publishers, a division of The Random House Group Limited. Also reprinted by permission of PFD on behalf of John McCarthy and Jill Morrell © as printed in the original volume.

Meeting God at Every Turn by Catherine Marshall. Reproduced by permission of Hodder and Stoughton Limited.

On Being a Jewish Christian by Hugh Montefiore. Reproduced by permission of Hodder and Stoughton Limited.

Angels: True Stories of How They Touch Our Lives by Hope Price, published by Macmillan. Reproduced by permission of Pan Macmillan.

The Mystics Come to Harley Street by Basil Douglas Smith, published by Regency Press. Reproduced by permission.

I Am With You Always: True Stories of Encounters with Jesus by G. Scott Sparrow, published by Macmillan. Reproduced by permission of Pan Macmillan.

So You're Lonely by Roy Trevivian, published by Fount. Reproduced by permission.

The Significance of Silence by Leslie Weatherhead, published by Epworth Press. Copyright © Trustees for Methodist Church Purposes. Used by permission of Methodist Publishing House.

Every effort has been made to trace the owners of copyright material. We apologize for any errors or omissions that may remain, and would ask those concerned to contact the publishers, who will ensure that full acknowledgement is made in future editions.

Introduction

A man is driving along a road at night. He notices the cats-eyes glowing red. As he slows down to take a closer look, he rounds the next bend – and finds an upturned vehicle on his side of the road. The warning prevented a serious accident.

A woman is sitting quietly at home when an angel appears in front of her. Without words, it conveys a message that is deeply reassuring. She is not religious, has never thought about angels before, and is sure it was not a dream.

A child is walking in the countryside with her family. She stops to look at a field of corn. Then feels the presence of someone else – 'so kind, so loving, so bright, so commanding' – enfolding her with light.

This book is about experiences which are out of the ordinary and which leave people with the impression that there's something else – a good something else – at work in the world, with which they have come into contact. These experiences, sometimes termed 'numinous', 'transcendent', 'religious' or 'mystical', have been happening since earliest times. They happen to people of all ages and different cultures, to people of deep religious faith and to people of none. They strike at times of crisis, and out of the blue; at times of soul-searching, and at times of nothing-particular-going-on.

The experiences are life-changing. They remain deeply embedded in people's memories, even if they rarely talk about them. They may leave people with the feeling that they are loved and valued, with a new sense of the importance of relationships or a renewed spiritual awareness.

This book offers a selection of experiences which people have described at different times. Some are taken from published accounts, others were related to me personally. I have gathered them loosely into topics but make no attempt to analyse or explain the stories told. People speak for themselves and I've been privileged to listen, read and learn.

The scientific study of 'religious experiences' is relatively new and straddles the fields of psychology, philosophy, religion and science. The reading list at the back of the book charts my own brief journey through some of them – a journey which led me over vast, rich landscapes crossed by ancient footpaths, some well trodden and others all but overgrown. At the end of my journey it was as if I were looking out over a vast ocean which laps at the edge of the world, holding the continents in place. An 'ocean of light and love', full of movement and luminescence, shooting stars and leaping fish.

If this selection encourages anyone to explore the landscape further, to delve more deeply into the mystery at work in the world and find, as St Angela of Foligno did, that 'this whole world is full of God', its task will be complete.

Madeleine Hill

I saw also that there was an ocean of darkness and death, but an infinite ocean of light and love, which flowed over the ocean of darkness.

George Fox (1624–90)

1

This whole world is full of God!

Awe and wonder in everyday life

The natural world has always been a source of awe and wonder. Artists, poets and musicians are inspired by the beauty of it. Scientists marvel at the order and complexity underlying it. Many of us head to the countryside when we feel in need of a recharge.

But while many people find nature awe-inspiring, some claim to have encountered a different level of reality while out in the countryside. Suddenly, it seems, the world is illuminated, lit up from within. They sense they are not alone, but accompanied by a presence – a presence both awesome and intimate, holy and yet deeply kind. They feel connected to the source of the universe; everything is one and everything is 'all right'.

'Awe and wonder' experiences don't only happen in beautiful places. They can also strike in the middle of an ordinary day. At the kitchen sink or travelling on a bus. Opening a cupboard or sitting in a chair. Without warning, awareness is heightened and the world is cast in a different light. These experiences may last only a few minutes but they have a timeless quality.

Is this what the Bible means when it speaks of the glory of God? Moses was minding his sheep in the hills when he encountered this glory shining out of a burning bush. It knew him intimately, addressed him by name and had a message for him. Moses took off his shoes and hid his face – he knew he was on holy ground. Jacob experienced the same quality of holiness in a dream while sleeping under the stars. He woke shaken to the core, declaring: 'Surely the Lord is in this place – and I did not know it!'

Is the glory of God all around us, in our homes, on our city streets, in our workplaces even? Does familiarity blind us to the possibility of wonder? Maybe, like Jacob, we could find that 'This is none other than the house of God, and this is the gate of heaven' (Genesis 28.17). How would we feel if we saw each moment and the events of all our lives as the place where God works and the gateway to eternity?

> *Heaven and earth are full of your glory.*
> *Hosanna in the highest!*
> Anglican service book

Enjoying the moment

Paul Hawker describes a moment of insight during a mountain hike.

The mountain I was standing on was completely surrounded by a plain of fluffy, corrugated clouds stretching dozens of kilometers off into the distance . . . Standing on the edge of the precipice, I had no land reference points. It was as if I was standing on the clouds themselves, an angel in heaven. I watched the setting sun cast colors onto my clouds – pinks, then golds with purples out on the far edges. It was so beautiful I held my breath so as to capture the consummate peace of this exquisite moment.

There was no great voice, no burning bush, but internally something 'clicked'. I had a deep, clear sense, a fragment of awareness, that all before me had been created, and that this creation somehow accommodated me. I too was part of it. The essence that had brought all this into being also included me. I, what lay before me, and its creator, were part of the same entity.

A warm feeling grew inside me, a knowing that I was *enjoyed* as much as I was *enjoying* the moment. It is as clear to me now as it was all those decades ago.

Paul Hawker, *Secret Affairs of the Soul*

An encounter with holiness

For this man, an 'inner prompting' led to an experience he found both terrifying and uplifting.

One evening as I lay down to sleep I was suddenly aware of a most strange sensation of awe, fear, almost unbearable excitement, and I wondered if I was going to find myself in the next world. But of course I wasn't, and next morning I had to get up and get on with my life.

Almost a fortnight later . . . I nodded off in an easy chair by the open window and awoke with the sun streaming down on my face – just enjoying doing nothing in particular, listening to the birds singing. But suddenly I became aware again of that strange mixture of fear and uplift entering my mind; and I sat there deeply puzzled for some minutes. Finally it became so insistent that I *had* to find out what it meant.

I walked up the passage to my bedroom, went down on my knees and asked for an explanation. As I did so, the glory of the universe shone before me – I was blinded by the dazzling white light. In my heart I flung my arms before my eyes, because I knew then that man could not look upon God and live. I was both terrified and yet uplifted – I can't explain it. I was shattered and then knew that I was a nothing. All my conceit and personal esteem vanished.

So great and awful was the Holiness that stood before me that I feared that it should ever happen again. But it completely changed my life. When I hear men in their folly say, 'You can't prove that there is a God!' I reply: 'You wait until He has taken half a step towards you and you are left in no doubt.' Why this happened to me, I can't understand. It may have been to arm

and stiffen me for what was coming; for our world was about
to collapse about our ears.

Gerald Priestland, The Case Against God

A great feeling of ecstasy

*Seeing something beautiful – a blackberry bush laden with fruit
– was the trigger for this experience.*

One day years ago I went for a walk in the fields with my dog.
My mind suddenly started thinking about the beauty around
me, and I considered the marvellous order and timing of all the
growth of each flower, herb and the abundance of all the visible
growth going on around. I remember thinking 'Here is mind'.
Then we had to get over a stile and suddenly I was confronted
with a bramble bush which was absolutely laden with black
glistening fruit. And the impact of that, linked with my former
reasoning, gave me a great feeling of ecstasy. For a few moments
I really did feel at one with the Universe or the Creative Power
we recognize. I know it was a feeling of oneness with something
outside myself, and also within. I must have been confronted
with the source of all being, whatever one should call it. I have
often told my friends about it, though it seems too sacred to talk
about. The experience has never been forgotten. It was quite
electric and quite unsought.

David Hay with Rebecca Nye, The Spirit of the Child

Everything is all right

'Awe and wonder' experiences happen to children, too.

My father used to take all the family for a walk on Sunday
evenings. On one such walk, we wandered across a narrow path
through a field of high, ripe corn. I lagged behind, and found
myself alone. Suddenly, heaven blazed on me. I was enveloped

in golden light. I was conscious of a presence, so kind, so loving, so bright, so consoling, so commanding, existing apart from me but so close. I heard no sound. But words fell into my mind quite clearly – 'Everything is all right. Everybody will be all right.'

David Hay, *Religious Experience Today*

A protective and loving presence

This child also felt there was something or someone very kind behind all the beauty of nature.

The dew on the grass seemed to sparkle like iridescent jewels in the sunlight, and the shadows of the house and trees seemed friendly and protective. In the heart of the child that I was, there seemed suddenly to well up a deep and overwhelming sense of gratitude, a sense of unending peace and security which seemed to be part of the beauty of the morning, the love and protection of my home and the sheer joy of being alive. I did not associate this with God, but I knew that in all this beauty was a friendliness, a protective and loving presence which included all that I had ever loved and yet was something much more.

Timothy Beardsworth, *A Sense of Presence*

A divine appointment

Leslie Weatherhead (1893–1976) was a popular Methodist minister and writer, with a keen insight into the links between psychological and Christian understandings.

I was staying at Jordans in Buckinghamshire, that lovely, secluded Quaker settlement, with its old-world garden, its ancient barn built from the timbers of the Mayflower, and its sense of quietude. It always seems like Sunday afternoon at Jordans.

One September morning I got up at a quarter to seven, walked through the kitchen garden, up through the orchard where the owls were still crying, through a gate and into a meadow. But not only into a meadow, into a great silence. It was in the meadow that I met God. The ground was so drenched with dew that it looked as if it were covered with hoar frost. The sun was peeping over the horizon, throwing long shadows upon the grass. It was an hour of bewitching loveliness. Magic was in the air and awe in my heart. One had that strange impression, which probably you have had many times, that one was being allowed to be present just as God had concluded the creation of the world, that one was seeing the world all new and fresh from His hand. There was a solemn hush which seemed to fall over the whole field and everything in it.

In a way it was a strange experience. One doesn't plan such hours of insight when one goes for a summer holiday. Yet at the end of that holiday, having done perhaps all the things one planned to do, the thing that stands out most is an hour of silence when the soul was caught up in rapturous worship and allowed to behold part of the beauty of God. You know that God is near, that He is speaking to you, that He has brought you to that hour and to that place, in order to say things to you in the silence that otherwise you would not stay to hear.

Leslie Weatherhead, *The Significance of Silence*

Getting supper ready

This writer's experience took place, if not at the kitchen sink, then very close by.

I went as usual to get a supper tray ready, and had opened the cupboard door, when I was suddenly invaded and surrounded by an awareness of God's love for me.

I realised this was Eternal Life. I knew what transfiguration meant – to glow with the knowledge of God's love.

I was told that I was part of the plan, and was shown a diagrammatic picture of the plan – the solid earth, and the curtain separating us from the people who have 'put on immortality'.

The kitchen faded away during this experience.

Basil Douglas Smith, *The Mystics Come to Harley Street*

Miracle on a bus

A miracle on public transport? Why not? The quiet confidence of this writer suggests a deep inner change took place.

The greatest gift I have ever been given and experienced was Everlasting Life. I was just given it while travelling on a bus, and it was a wonderful joy and came as a ray from outside. I looked to see if other people had seen or understood anything, but all was normal and I just wondered how or why I had received such a marvellous revelation.

Timothy Beardsworth, *A Sense of Presence*

Intense love for strangers

The bus was the scene for this encounter, too.

I was travelling in a bus, and the experience lasted only for a few seconds.

There were three vivid impressions.

The first was of a great brightness; the second was like a flash of insight during which I seemed to understand the nature of things, knew that it was good, and that all was well; and the third was a feeling that I was a vessel into which a great love was flowing from the centre of the brightness. As the experience left me, and I became aware again of the other passengers, I felt an intense love for them all, although they were complete strangers to me.

I would say I felt the presence of God.

Basil Douglas Smith, *The Mystics Come to Harley Street*

An inward state of peace and joy

John Trevor describes an important moment in his life.

One brilliant Sunday morning, my wife and boys went to the
Unitarian Chapel in Macclesfield. I felt it impossible to accom-
pany them – as though to leave the sunshine on the hills, and go
down there to the chapel, would be for the time an act of spiritual suicide. And I felt such need for new inspiration and expan-
sion in my life. So, very reluctantly and sadly, I left my wife and
boys to go down into the town, while I went further up into the
hills with my stick and my dog. In the loveliness of the morning, and the beauty of the hills and valleys, I soon lost my sense
of sadness and regret. For nearly an hour I walked along the
road to the 'Cat and Fiddle', and then returned. On the way
back, suddenly, without warning, I felt that I was in Heaven –
an inward state of peace and joy and assurance indescribably
intense, accompanied with a sense of being bathed in a warm
glow of light, as though the external condition had brought
about the internal effect – a feeling of having passed beyond the
body, though the scene around me stood out more clearly and
as if nearer to me than before, by reason of the illumination in
the midst of which I seemed to be placed. This deep emotion
lasted, though with decreasing strength, until I reached home,
and for some time after, only gradually passing away.

John Trevor, *My Quest for God*

Holy ground

Moses was keeping the flock of his father-in-law Jethro, the
priest of Midian; he led his flock beyond the wilderness, and
came to Horeb, the mountain of God. There the angel of the
Lord appeared to him in a flame of fire out of a bush; he looked,
and the bush was blazing, yet it was not consumed. Then Moses
said, 'I must turn aside and look at this great sight, and see why
the bush is not burned up.' When the Lord saw that he had

turned aside to see, God called to him out of the bush, 'Moses! Moses!' And he said, 'Here I am.' Then he said, 'Come no closer! Remove the sandals from your feet, for the place on which you are standing is holy ground.' He said further, 'I am the God of your father, the God of Abraham, the God of Isaac, and the God of Jacob.' And Moses hid his face, for he was afraid to look at God.

Exodus 3.1–6

2

All night, all day

Angels watching over us?

———◦◦◦◦———

You don't have to look far to see evidence of angel belief in our society – even if much of that evidence dates from the past. From the winged stone creatures that brood over graveyards and church interiors to place names like Angel and Los Angeles, it's clear that angels have played an important part in the Western psyche. More recently there's been an upsurge of angel interest, expressed in books, training courses, internet sites and structures like the huge steel Angel of the North.

Angels have been important in many of the world's great religions and mythologies. In the Bible they are God's messengers, appearing at moments of special significance to guide, save or encourage individuals. Angels are alive and well in the New Testament and in early Christian belief. Somewhere along the way they were relegated to the realms of fairytale and folklore, which may be why many of us have never seriously considered that they could be anything other than symbolic.

And yet many people today are convinced they have seen angels. Some appear as traditional figures in wings and white robes. Others look ordinary in every way – until they vanish into thin air after performing their work of rescue or encouragement. Another order of angels is felt physically as a hand on the shoulder pulling people back from danger or death.

There have been many published accounts of angel sightings in recent years. I've limited this chapter to examples of some of the ways in which angels are most often experienced. They are

13

offered as a possibility, a glimmer of a suggestion that perhaps, behind all that our rational minds can grasp and reduce to our size, there is more. An order of beings who come only when we really need them and are discerned only by those who are ready to acknowledge them. A realm of the spirit which the ancients perceived and the Bible takes for granted and about which we could, if we were so inclined, keep an open mind?

> *All night, all day,*
> *angels watchin' over me, my Lord!*
> Negro Spiritual

Angel on duty

Angels are often seen in hospitals. This man was by his wife's bed in intensive care when both he and his son had their sighting.

Suddenly, through my tears, I saw what I thought to be a figure, an angel, behind the bed rails – I ignored it, thinking it was [brought about by] exhaustion and anxiety. A few minutes later I looked to see my son staring at the same spot – he turned to me and asked if I too could see an angel behind the bed. That moment the staff nurse was passing the foot of the bed and I turned and asked her if she could see anything other than us in the cubicle – the nurse smiled and told us not to presume it meant the worst. She acted as if this was a normal occurrence. I turned back to my wife and watched the figure melt away. Literally from that moment on my wife regained consciousness.

Emma Heathcote-James, *Seeing Angels*

Ministering angels

Sadly, Eric has died since he told me his story, but he never forgot the angels he saw as a young child.

It happened on 14 August 1918 but my memory is as clear as if it happened yesterday. I was five, we were living in Writhlington, outside Radstock. My grandma had 11 children – the youngest, Ken, was 11. Ken and I were great friends, like brothers, though he was my uncle. He went down with diphtheria and wasn't expected to live. The doctor had given up hope.

They lived half a mile away from us. This particular morning, my mother and I were going up to see him. (My mother had been the evening before. She knew he was very ill.) It was 11 o'clock, a fine August morning. Outside our house was a 40-acre meadow with a spinney of beech trees at the top. We got outside our gate and were walking up the road. I said 'What are those, Mother?' In front of the beech trees there were four winged figures playing in front of the trees. Their wings were silver, they were hovering in the air and flying in and out of the trees. My mother saw them, too. She said, 'What do they look like?' I said, 'Angels.' She said, 'I expect they've come for Uncle Ken.'

We got to my grandma's house and she said, 'He's gone.'

The trees are still there. Every time I see them I wonder if I'll ever see the angels again. It didn't seem strange to me, or to my mother, to see angels, though we'd never seen them before and I've never seen any since. We believed people had guardian angels. If I were an artist I could paint what I saw, they were so clear and distinct.

Bedside angel

A traditional angel with wings comforted Maggie as she lay awake at night, terrified by stories her brother had told to scare her. It started with a glow at the foot of her bed:

I watched, fascinated as it grew. The glow spread until it was huge, stretching up as high as the ceiling and as wide as my bed. Slowly and quietly the figure of an angel appeared in the middle of the glow. I had the most wonderful feeling of safety and well-being. The angel was beautiful, all in sparkling white, with a lovely kind smiling face, golden hair and a pair of huge wings which swept up and curved over his back, sleek with white feathers.

I don't know how long he stayed, but the next thing I remember was my mother coming into the room, giving me a smack and thrusting me back into bed. I told her I was looking for angel feathers on the floor, which got me another smack. I was then left alone in the dark, but now it didn't matter because I had seen an angel. I knew Jesus had sent him and I was safe.

Hope Price, *Angels*

Sheets of blue light

Valerie's angel seemed to convey a message to her.

About ten years ago I was sitting quietly. I was not ill. I had nothing in particular to worry me. I was not asleep. What I saw and felt was nothing like a dream. I felt that I was looking into a cave made of sheets of blue light. I felt as if I was moving towards the cave. Then I realised it was not a cave but a winged being. What I had taken to be a cave was in fact huge wings made of sheets of blue light, like feathers. I was not moving towards it at all – in fact, it was moving towards me, to enfold me in its wings.

I heard no voice, but a strong message on what I can only call a flow of 'love'. The message was that everything is 'alright'. Everything in some way was in order and will work out all right in the end – not just for me, but everything. Everything was a part of everything else. All is one.

I have no religious faith. I had never thought about winged beings or angels before this . . . Only this year (1998) I noticed a text in a church. It said 'All is well, all is well and all manner of things are well' (Julian of Norwich). That is more or less the message/feeling that I had.

Emma Heathcote-James, Seeing Angels

A guiding hand

Michael (14) left it late to cycle home from a friend's house, accidentally leaving his lights and reflective strip behind.

Realising how late I was, and knowing I was in trouble, especially if the police spotted me without lights, I decided to take a quicker, quieter route along the canal towpath. Almost at once I knew I had made a stupid decision as the path was ill-lit and very rough, so I found my bike bouncing around and coming dangerously close to the foul-looking water. Too scared to get off and walk, for the place looked so eerie at night, I tried to pedal faster. My heart was pounding and I was very conscious of the wall which fell away steeply to the canal on my left, especially as I am a very poor swimmer. Perspiration trickled down my back with fear.

Suddenly, I felt the handlebars of my bike turn severely to the right, forcing me to ride into the side of the bank with such speed that I went up it a little way, before descending again to the path some yards ahead. The bike was not under my control, I merely sat with my hands holding the handlebars, being directed by the force. At last I reached the end of the tow-path and was once more on a road with lighting, feeling safe. I stopped pedalling to catch my breath, my heart still beating strongly, and tried to work out what had happened. At this point a neighbour appeared, walking the family dog. Recognising me he said, 'What are you doing? Isn't it time you were home?' Seeing I had no lights he said, 'I'll walk back with you. You'd be better off pushing your bike without lights. And it's a good job you didn't take the tow-path.' When I asked why, he said that a large hole had appeared about halfway along the path due to a collapsed drain, dangerous in day-time but lethal at night.

Glennyce Eckersley, *An Angel at my Shoulder*

An angel in the garage

Graham and Sandra had been planning a diving trip, but Sandra felt unwell, so they decided Graham would go alone.

Taking a packed lunch, Graham went into the garage to load the car with his equipment. The kitchen had a door leading directly into the garage, and he went in and out several times, lifting things he would need into the car. Finally he said goodbye, feeling a little guilty but eager to dive. He stepped into the garage, closing the door behind him. On approaching the car, with his keys ready, he suddenly felt a hand on his shoulder. Turning round, he expected to find Sandra holding some item he'd forgotten, but there was no one there.

Standing there for a moment perplexed, he nevertheless ended up deciding that he had imagined the sensation.

Graham went towards the car once more, intending to open the door and drive away, but once again the hand fell on his shoulder. As before he turned around to find nothing, until the darkened garage started to fill with light, so bright and yet so soft that he knew something supernatural was happening. Hurrying through the door back into the house, he called Sandra to tell her what had happened but there was no response. Dashing into the lounge, he saw her slumped on the floor, her face as white as a sheet. His heart pounding, he felt

18

for a pulse. To his immense relief she was still alive. He quickly called for help and in only minutes, although the wait seemed like hours, they were on the way to hospital.

On arrival it was discovered that Sandra had suffered a stroke, and Graham was told that the speed at which she had been admitted to hospital had been very much in her favour. Sandra made an excellent recovery. Graham mulls over daily the events of that Saturday morning, with awe and wonder. He is not, nor ever has been, a religious man, but it had obviously been a case of intervention by an angel, without whose help Sandra would surely have died. Graham says that he wishes he could thank the angel with all his heart, but that, being an angel, he's sure he knows.

Glennyce Eckersley, *An Angel at my Shoulder*

Entertaining angels unawares

Was the meter reader who called on Isabel an angel? As she struggled to work full time, care for a family and study to be a lay preacher, she felt in need of encouragement.

One day when she was at home trying to write an essay with a migraine coming on, Isabel felt tired and fed up. She put on some background music to help her concentration. Just then a uniformed official of the Midland Electricity Board arrived to read the meter.

Isabel invited him in and offered him some coffee. While sitting in the kitchen drinking the coffee he noticed that the music playing was from Taizé, a Christian community in France, who have a unique style of singing. In a soft Irish accent, he said he had spent time in the Veritas Community in Ireland, similar to Taizé, which he described as 'next to heaven'.

They talked for some time, having a great deal in common and each talking about their relationship with the Lord. He stressed to her the importance of prayer for all who wished to move on with God. The conversation with this gentle middle-aged man with twinkling eyes left Isabel feeling better and much refreshed. She explains, 'He smiled, shook my hand and left. Then I remembered that he had not read the meter, so I went next door, but he wasn't there. The other neighbours had not seen him either, and none of them had had their meters read that day. There was no van or electricity man anywhere about. This man had led me back to God, which I needed. We had talked about Jesus, and his coffee cup was empty. Yet no one else had seen him. Was he an angel? I most surely say he was.'

Hope Price, *Angels*

Guardian angel

Freda believes the young man who helped her must be her guardian angel. Her pastor tells the story.

Freda was driving along a city highway when she started to feel ill. Fearing she might pass out, she pulled up at the side of the road – right alongside a young man who was hitchhiking. He was good looking, and was dressed in a black leather jacket. Freda picked him up, saying, 'I am feeling very ill. If you could drive me across town to my doctor's surgery, I'll make sure you get a lift anywhere you want to go.' The young man agreed, and drove her to her doctor's. He helped her out of the car and into the clinic, where a nurse took her into one of the examination rooms. A few minutes later Freda realised she had forgotten to thank the young man and arrange for him to get his lift. She went back to the reception area and asked the receptionist where he had gone. 'What young man?' asked the receptionist. 'The one who practically carried me in here,' replied Freda. 'No one carried you in here! You came in yourself and put your keys on the counter.'

Freda thought she must be ill indeed. She imagined the whole thing had been a hallucination. About a year later, she was shopping in a large mall during the Christmas season. It was late opening, and she came out just as the stores were closing. Freda had parked her car in an underground car park next to the store; her car was in the very last space in the far corner, next to the concrete wall. The space next to her car was empty.

As Freda began to walk to her car, she heard footsteps on her right. Looking up, she saw a man walking towards her – there was no one else around. She quickened her pace – the man quickened his. She began to run, and so did he. As she ran, she fumbled in her bag for her keys, but when she reached her car, realised she wouldn't have time to open the door before the man reached her. She turned to face him, and as she did so, saw him stop about thirty feet from her with a terrified look in his eyes. Abruptly, he turned round and ran out of the car park.

Freda turned back to her car. There, standing between the cement wall and her car was the young man she had picked up a year before. He was wearing the same leather jacket and was smiling at her. She glanced over her shoulder to make sure her attacker had gone, and when she turned back to thank the young man, he had vanished. She walked all round the car. There was no door in the wall. He had simply vanished. Once again, he had saved her life. Freda then knew she had been visited by an angel.

Jack Deere, *Surprised by the Voice of God* (altered)

A playful angel

Johnny was born with Down's syndrome. One night his father, Gene, heard a noise coming from his bedroom.

I immediately went to check on him. When I opened the door, I discovered not one, but two baby boys sitting in Johnny's crib. They were playing a game known only to them and squealing with laughter. The other baby turned toward me, looked into my eyes with a piercing glance, then suddenly disappeared.

21

To this day I believe with all my heart that God allowed me to see Johnny's guardian angel momentarily in order to encourage me for the years that lay ahead.

Jack Deere, *Surprised by the Voice of God*

The man who lifted the lorry

This story was told by a doctor, Judith, about her time as a medical student in London.

It was nearly forty years ago and I was working as a third-year medical student in the casualty department of St Mary's Hospital, Paddington. I was an atheist, a typical student of the time, and working with me was another student, Jenny. Anyone less fanciful than Jenny is hard to imagine. She was a healthy, hearty woman who had played lacrosse for Roedean.

A young child was brought in on a stretcher. She was unconscious and accompanied by her very distressed parents, a policeman, and a bystander at the time. Lucy had run into the middle of the busy Edgware Road and a lorry had hit her and then the wheels had gone over her – not just once but twice – the rear as well. The policeman who had been on duty had watched it happen.

Together with the doctor on duty, the three of us examined the unconscious child. Apart from one small bruise on her shoulder she was totally unmarked. We were about to send her off for X-rays, when she opened her eyes and smiled. 'Where is that man in white?' she demanded. The doctor came forward. 'No – no,' said Lucy, 'the man in the long shiny dress.' We held her hands and stroked her face. 'The man did that,' said Lucy, 'He stroked my face, as he picked up the wheels. The wheels did not touch me,' she added.

Lucy then fell into a totally normal, deep sleep. A full medical examination revealed not a single injury, except for the small bruise. The following day, Lucy was discharged. The lorry driver swore that he had felt two bumps and had vomited in the road at the sight of the unconscious Lucy. Lucy herself retained a child's quiet unconcern and the certainty that 'the man in white had lifted the lorry'.

Emma Heathcote-James, *Seeing Angels*

Surrounded by angels

The Indian mystic Sadhu Sundar Singh (1889–1929) relates his angel experience almost in passing.

A few months ago I was lying alone in my room suffering acutely from an ulcer in my eye. The pain was so great that I could do no other work, so I spent the time in prayer and intercession. One day I had been thus engaged for only a few minutes when the spiritual world was opened to me and I found myself surrounded by numbers of angels. Immediately I forgot all my pain . . . I asked: 'Do the angels and saints always look upon the face of God, and if they see Him in what form does He appear?'

One of the saints said: 'As the sea is full of water, so is the whole universe filled with God . . . Because He is infinite, His children, who are finite, can see Him only in the form of Christ.'

C. F. Andrew, *Sadhu Sundar Singh*

An angelic messenger

After the sabbath, as the first day of the week was dawning, Mary Magdalene and the other Mary went to see the tomb. And suddenly there was a great earthquake; for an angel of the Lord, descending from heaven, came and rolled back the stone and sat on it. His appearance was like lightning, and his clothing white as snow. For fear of him the guards shook and became like dead men. But the angel said to the women, 'Do not be afraid; I know that you are looking for Jesus who was crucified. He is not here; for he has been raised, as he said. Come, see the place where he lay. Then go quickly and tell his disciples, "He has been raised from the dead, and indeed he is going ahead of you to Galilee; there you will see him." This is my message for you.' So they left the tomb quickly with fear and great joy, and ran to tell his disciples.

Matthew 28.1–8

3

Approaching the gates

What is dying like?

———————

What happens when we die? It's the final mystery, the one the greatest human minds are powerless to fathom. And perhaps a cause of fear, as the time for our own death or the deaths of people we love draws closer.

The study of 'near-death experiences' is relatively recent, although there are stories of such experiences going back many centuries. They mark a distinction between *clinical* death, when all vital signs are absent, and *biological* death, which is irreversible. There's remarkable consistency between them. They affect those who go through them deeply, often changing their view of life profoundly, sometimes making it hard to relate to those who haven't shared the experience.

Scientific opinion is split on near-death experiences. While some neuro-scientists attribute them to the activity of dying brain cells, others find that explanation implausible. But there's a growing interest in them, together with a recognition of the importance of the 'spiritual' in both medical and psychological circles. One thing is certain. Those approaching death *from the inside* feel very different from those looking on. For the great majority of those who survive to describe it the experience is one of joy, freedom and peace.

Is it possible that the passage from life to death is attended with the same tender devotion that some people believe accompanies us each moment of our lives? Those whose stories are included in this chapter would say so. Thousands more from all parts of the globe would echo that belief. Others have had special experiences as their loved ones made the journey and their stories are told in a later chapter.

It is a great thing to see what is waiting for us there and to know where we are going to live.

St Teresa of Avila

Every single shimmer

Many near-death experiences start with feeling 'out of the body', with a very clear view of everything around.

I was hovering over a stretcher in one of the emergency rooms at the hospital. I glanced down at the stretcher, knew the body wrapped in blankets was mine, and really didn't care. The room was much more interesting than my body. And what a neat perspective. I could see everything. And I do mean everything! I could see the top of the light on the ceiling, and the underside of the stretcher. I could see the tiles on the ceiling and the tiles on the floor, simultaneously. Three hundred sixty degree spherical vision. And not just spherical. Detailed! I could see every single hair and the follicle out of which it grew on the head of the nurse standing beside the stretcher. At the time I knew exactly how many hairs there were to look at. But I shifted focus. She was wearing glittery white nylons. Every single shimmer and sheen stood out in glowing detail, and once again I knew exactly how many sparkles there were.

Kenneth Ring and Sharon Cooper, *Mindsight*

Pictures of my life

Time seemed to expand and lengthen for this Austrian climber while he was plunging towards his likely death after falling, though in fact he was unharmed.

I still grasp completely what is happening, am fully conscious of what is going on round me: I am brought up short for a moment. I register: the first piton has gone. The second. I strike against the rock, scrape against it as I go down, want to resist, to claw at it. But a wild power dashes me inexorably down and down. Lost. Finished.

But now I am not frightened any more. Fear of death leaves me. All feeling, every perception is snuffed out. Only more emptiness, complete resignation within me and night round me. I am not plummeting downwards any more, either. I am sinking softly through space on a cloud, resigned, released. Have I already passed the gateway to the kingdom of shadows? Suddenly light and movement enter the darkness round me. Cloudy figures detach themselves from me and become clearer and clearer. A film flickers on to a screen inside me: I see myself in it again, see myself, only three years old, tottering to the grocer's shop next door. In my hand I am clutching the penny that my mother had given me so that I could buy myself a few sweets. Then I see myself as an older child, see how my right leg is caught under a falling layer of planks. My grandfather is trying to raise the planks. Mother is cooling and stroking my crushed foot . . . More and more pictures out of my life flicker up and are shaken into confusion. The film snaps. Chains of light cut through the empty black background like lightning. Catherine wheels, raining sparks, flickering will o' the wisps . . . Again I am standing in front of myself. I cannot recognize myself physically in this form, but I know that it is me. Suddenly a cry out of the distance: 'Hias!' and again 'Hias!' A call from within me? Suddenly sun-bathed rock and light and silence before me. My eyes have opened. The window into the past had been thrown open. Now it is shut again. And again the frightened cry. It comes from this world, from above . . . Now I become conscious for the first time that I have just survived a great fall, have returned from a long journey, back through my life, back from an earlier existence, have slipped into my skin again. I worked myself up the seventy feet with the help of the rope . . . The last piton had held.

Johann Christoph Hampe, To Die is Gain

Every single thing we did

Phyllis also has a review of her past life during her near-death experience.

And into this great peace that I had become there came the life of Phyllis parading past my view . . . The reliving included not only the deeds committed by Phyllis since her birth in 1937 in Twin Falls, Idaho, but also a reliving of every thought ever thought and every word ever spoken PLUS the effect of every thought, word and deed upon everyone and anyone who had ever come within her sphere of influence whether she actually knew them or not PLUS the effect of her every thought, word and deed upon the weather, the soil, plants and animals, the water, everything else . . . I never before realized that we were responsible and accountable for EVERY SINGLE THING WE DID. That was overwhelming!

It was me judging me, not some heavenly St Peter. And my judgment was critical and stern. I was not satisfied with many, many things Phyllis had done, said or thought. There was a feeling of sadness and failure, yet a growing feeling of joy when the realization came that Phyllis had always done SOMETHING . . . She tried. Much of what she did was constructive and positive. She learned and grew in her learning. This was satisfying. Phyllis was okay.

P. M. H. Atwater, I Died Three Times in 1977

A great hand of light

Many people meet a 'being of light' as they approach death. This Dutch woman recalls a childhood accident.

I was a ten-year-old girl. In summer my parents liked to go with me to the swimming pool on the river. The children's pool was lined with planks. I could easily stand in it, as I played with the other children. But once I slipped on the slippery floor. I went down immediately, came up again, lost my balance once more and went down again, this time completely. I don't know how long the drowning lasted, but I do know that I was fully conscious. Afterwards I was able to remember that I had passed some frontier and had entered into a new reality. Light in profusion shone round me. The main colour was red, passing into yellow and orange. When I say 'shone round me', I can remember it as being a reality which eluded the mode of our perception. It was perception, not as an objective registering, but – to take a German word – a *Wahr-Nehmen*, in the literal sense, a finding true, a being surrounded by something so loving and tender that even today I can find no words for it. 'I' remained present, completely conscious, and simply put myself, if I may so express it, into this great hand of light . . . until my mother drew me up by the hair. It was a long time before I could overcome the disappointment at being again 'this side' of the frontier and at being taken away from that light. I was quite unable to feel grateful to my mother.

Johann Christoph Hampe, *To Die is Gain*

Total, unconditional love

Nel describes how she felt in the presence of the light.

Suddenly, I became aware of a light. It was all around me, it enveloped me, it completely surrounded me. It was an unearthly kind of light. It had color that is unmatched here on earth. It was not a beam of sunlight; it was not the glow from a 100-watt bulb; it was not a roaring fire; it was not a host of candles; it was not a celestial explosion in the midnight sky.

It was warm; it was radiant; it was peaceful; it was accepting; it was forgiving; it was completely nonjudgmental; and it gave me a sense of total security the likes of which I had never known. I loved it. It was perfection; it was total, unconditional love. It was anything and everything you would wish for on earth. It was all there, in the Light.

Kenneth Ring and Evelyn Elsaesser Valarino,
Lessons from the Light

The garden where beauty found its name

David describes in detail the beautiful place which was part of his experience. This is all the more surprising because he awoke from his coma blind and paralysed having suffered severe brain damage.

It was then that the Lord took me by the hand and led me through a garden where surely beauty had found its name. This was an old-fashioned, typically English garden with a lush green velvet lawn, bounded by deep curving borders brimming with flowers, each flower nestling within its family group, each group proclaiming its presence with a riot of colour and fragrance as if blessed by a morning dew. The entrance to the garden was marked by a trellis of honeysuckle so laden that you had to crouch down to pass beneath while at the other end a rustic garden gate led to the outside. It was here that my walk through was to end as I was gently led through to the other side. It was at this moment that the realization that I was going to live came to me and I would have to face the consequences of living. There followed two weeks as I lay in a coma in an in-between world.

Peter Fenwick and Elizabeth Fenwick, *The Truth in the Light*

Face to face with my friend

Like many others who have near-death experiences, George met a friend who had died several years before.

First the Light was apparent to me, and then what was apparent was the tunnel I was in that was gray and white. But it had none of the things you associate with something like that. Rather than being cold, it was warm. It was beautiful. I was going to that Light. That's where I was headed. It was just a feeling of total, total love that enveloped me. As I say, I was headed toward the Light and that's where I wanted to go. It was fantastic.

In the short period of time that I was there – although I had no concept of time while I was in there – but anyway, before I made it to the Light, the next thing I knew I was standing in front of a guy. He looked at me, I looked at him, and he was a friend of mine.

Tom just looked at me and said, 'You've got to go back, George. It's not your time yet.' He looked great. When Tom was alive, he was bald and he was so thin. And now he had hair. He never had hair when he was here.

Mally Cox-Chapman, *Glimpses of Heaven*

Early morning, on a beach

A clergyman felt intense sadness on coming back to life.

I lay there, fully conscious, and noticed my heartbeat becoming slower and slower; I was just waiting for it to stop altogether. But I experienced something else at the same time. I was standing on a beach, in the early morning. It was absolutely still; I only faintly heard the splashing of the water on the beach. A thick but shining mist lay over everything, and I waited in intense expectation, for I knew that the mist would soon rise and then I would see Him, there in the light . . . Then it was as if something inside me had turned over, my heart beat more strongly, and everything had gone. Now coming back to life seemed agony and disappointment, and this feeling persisted for many years.

Quoted in Johann Christoph Hampe, *To Die is Gain*

Touching the bright, sparkling fringe

The writer and New Testament scholar J. B. Phillips describes his experience in detail.

I had been ill for months, forced to resign my first job through ill-health. I lay in hospital, exhausted after a severe and prolonged operation. Physically I was weaker than I had thought it possible for a human being to be and yet remain conscious. I could hear and see, but I could not so much as move a finger nor blink an eyelid by any effort of the will. Yet my mind was perfectly clear, and late one night I overheard a doctor murmur to the night nurse: 'I am afraid he won't live till the morning.'

In my state of exhaustion this aroused no emotion at all, but I remember making a mental note that patients who are gravely ill and apparently unconscious may yet be able to hear.

I would not say that I felt then the presence of God as a person, I knew Him rather as some kind of 'dimension'. I was a helpless human being resting entirely upon my Creator. God seemed to be, as it were, the sea of being, supporting me. I felt that God to be infinitely compassionate and infinitely kind.

I fell asleep. Immediately, as it seemed, I had this vivid dream.

I was alone, depressed and miserable, trudging down a dusty slope. Around me were the wrecks and refuse of human living. There were ruined houses, pools of stagnant water, cast-off shoes, rusty tin cans, worn-out tyres and rubbish of every kind.

As I picked my way through this dreary mess, I looked up. Not far away on the other side of a little valley, was a vista of indescribable beauty. It seemed as though all the loveliness of mountain and stream, of field and forest, of cloud and sky were displayed with such intensity of beauty that I gasped for breath. The loveliest of scents were wafted across to me. Heart-piercing bird-songs could be clearly heard. The whole vision seemed to promise the answer to my deepest longings as does the sight of water to a desperately thirsty man.

I ran towards this glorious world. I knew intuitively that there lay the answer to all my questing, the satisfaction for all that I had most deeply desired. This shining fresh world was the welcoming frontier of my true and permanent home.

I gathered my strength and hurried down the dirty, littered slope.

I noticed that only a tiny stream separated me from all that glory and loveliness. Even as I ran some little part of me realised, with a lifting of the heart, that Bunyan's 'icy river' was, as I had long suspected, only a figment of his imagination. For not only was the stream a very narrow one, but as I approached it, I found that a shining white bridge had been built across it.

I ran towards the bridge, but even as I was about to set foot on it, my heart full of expectant joy, a figure in white appeared before me. He seemed to me supremely gentle but absolutely authoritative. He looked at me smiling, gently shook his head, and pointed me back to the miserable slope down which I had so eagerly run.

I have never known such bitter disappointment, and although I turned obediently, I could not help bursting into tears. This passionate weeping must have awakened me, for the next thing I remember was the night-nurse bending over me and saying, rather reproachfully, 'What are you crying for? You've come through tonight – now you're going to live!'

What could I say to someone who had not seen what I had seen?

It is nearly forty years since the night of that dream, but it remains as true and as clear to me today as it was then. Words are almost useless as a means to describe what I saw and felt, even though I have attempted to use them.

I can only record my conviction that I saw reality that

night, the bright sparkling fringe of the world that is eternal.
The vision has never faded.

J. B. Phillips and Denis Duncan (eds),
Through the Year with J. B. Phillips

Departure point

The psychologist C. G. Jung described his near-death experience as one of the most meaningful events of his life.

It seemed to me that I was high up in space. Far below I saw the globe of the earth, bathed in a gloriously blue light. I saw the deep blue sea and the continents. Far below my feet lay Ceylon, and in the distance ahead of me the subcontinent of India. My field of vision did not include the whole earth, but its global shape was plainly distinguishable and its outlines shone with a silvery gleam through that wonderful blue light. In many places the globe seemed coloured, or spotted dark green like oxidized silver. Far away to the left lay a broad expanse – the reddish-yellow desert of Arabia: it was as though the silver of the earth had there assumed a reddish-gold hue. Then came the Red Sea, and far, far back – as if in the upper left of a map – I could just make out a bit of the Mediterranean. My gaze was directed chiefly toward that. Everything else appeared indistinct. I could also see the snow-covered Himalayas, but in that direction it was foggy or cloudy. I did not look to the right at all. I knew that I was on the point of departing from the earth.

Later I discovered how high in space one would have to be to have so extensive a view – approximately a thousand miles! The sight of the earth from this height was the most glorious thing I had ever seen.

C. G. Jung, *Memories, Dreams, Reflections*

Near-death experience?

I know a person in Christ who fourteen years ago was caught up to the third heaven – whether in the body or out of the body I do not know; God knows. And I know that such a person – whether in the body or out of the body I do not know; God knows – was caught up into Paradise and heard things that are not to be told, that no mortal is permitted to repeat. On behalf of such a one I will boast, but on my own behalf I will not boast, except of my weaknesses.

2 Corinthians 12.2–5

4

Messengers from heaven

Do people come back from the dead?

———◦◦◦◦———

Do people come back from the dead? After bereavement, it isn't unusual for people to feel that their loved one has communicated with them in some way. Perhaps the experience of loss heightens our sensitivity to an unusual level. Perhaps love truly does create a bond which is indissoluble.

Some people dismiss after-death appearances as wishful thinking, the products of minds in denial of the reality of loss. Others might associate them with spiritualism and other practices of trying to contact the dead which the Bible warns against. And whereas all churches take a serious view of death and dying, not all believe it is appropriate even to pray for 'the departed'.

Whatever our beliefs, the abrupt cutting of emotional ties leaves us bruised and traumatized. Yet repeatedly, and across cultures, people claim to have seen and communicated with loved ones after their deaths. Experiences they didn't look for and cannot explain. But which brought them great comfort and hope.

In one study, a doctor found that *nearly half* the widows and widowers who attended his surgery claimed to have seen their loved one at least once after death. In this chapter people relate how dead loved ones apparently came to help, guide and reassure those they had left behind. For my part, I found their stories heartening, an affirmation that God is the Lord of life and death and that times of heartbreak and loss can be times when he shows us his love in a specially tender and intimate way.

For life and death are one, even as the river and the sea are one.
Kahlil Gibran, *The Prophet*

Advance warning

When Jane Goodall's husband Derek died, her son (Grub) received advance warning.

At the time of Derek's illness, Grub, thirteen years old, was a boarder at a little preparatory school near Bournemouth. He did not know that Derek was close to death. Well, the night that Derek was dying, Grub was awakened from his sleep by a vivid dream. In his dream Olly arrived at the school and spoke to him. 'Grub, I have something very sad to tell you. Derek died last night.' He went to sleep again, but once more was awakened by the dream, and Olly again repeated her message. When it happened a third time he became distressed, and could not sleep. He actually went to the school matron to tell her he was having terrible nightmares, though he did not tell her what they were.

In the morning Olly arrived at the school . . . Olly took Grub outside into the garden and told him she had some sad news. 'I know,' he said. 'Derek is dead, isn't he.' Olly was stunned – until he told his dream.

Lulu, the same age as Grub at the time, suffered from Down's syndrome. Derek and I had been great friends with her parents and visited their house frequently . . . Derek was good with children, and Lulu loved him. The night he died, sometime in the small hours, she woke up and she ran along to where Mary, her nanny, was sleeping.

'Mary,' she said, urgently. 'Please wake up. That man has come and he likes me. He is smiling.' Mary, half roused, told Lulu she had been dreaming, and to go back to bed. But Lulu persisted. 'Please come, Mary. I want to show you. He is smiling.' In the end Mary sat up, resigned.

'Lulu, tell me who you mean. Who is this man who is smiling at you?'

'I don't remember his name,' said Lulu. 'But he comes with Jane, and he walks with a stick. And he likes me. He really likes me.'

Two children, in two parts of the world. Two children whom Derek had loved. It is so easy in a skeptical, reductionist scientific world to explain away these sorts of things as coincidental dreams, hallucinations or psychological reactions triggered by the onset of pain, stress or loss. But I have never been able to discount such experiences so easily.

Jane Goodall, *Reason for Hope*

Parting gift

Adele's nine-year-old son conveyed something very practical to her.

My son, Jeremy, died the day after Mother's Day. Three weeks later, just before I woke up, I heard him ask, 'What are you going to do with my money?' I said, 'What money?' And he said, 'All the money that you saved for me.' I had totally forgotten about Jeremy's savings account, and I didn't even know where he had hidden his savings book. I asked what he wanted me to do with it because obviously it must have been very important to him. Jeremy said, 'I want you to go see Malcolm.' Malcolm is a friend of mine who is a diamond wholesaler. I said, 'Well, whatever is in that account isn't enough to go see Malcolm!' And Jeremy replied, 'Yes it is! Just go see Malcolm, and you'll understand what I'm talking about. When you see it, you will know. You will think of me.' Then he was gone and I woke up.

Although I thought this was kind of crazy, I looked around the house for my son's savings book but couldn't find it. Several days later, I happened to be in the same building as Malcolm's wholesale jewelry store. So I popped in there and started looking around. I saw a beautiful butterfly necklace with a diamond in it. It suddenly clicked what Jeremy had said. 'You'll know it when you see it. It will remind you of me.' My heart started pounding and I got kind of nervous. I asked Malcolm how much the necklace would cost. After some figuring and some bantering back and forth, he told me $200. I told him I would come back later.

My heart was still pounding when I went back to my office and called the bank. I explained that I couldn't find my son's savings book and wanted to know how much money was in his account. In a few minutes, I was told the amount was $200.47! I went back to Malcolm's store after work and bought the butterfly necklace with Jeremy's money. Now I don't go anywhere without it. I can touch it and say, 'My son gave me this for my last Mother's Day with him!'

Kenneth Ring and Evelyn Elsaesser Valarino,
Lessons from the Light

Dream rescue

A young woman felt that her brother rescued her through a powerful dream.

It was a year and a half since my brother had died and I was having a dream one night. I dreamt I was with my friends in a hallway and one of my friends said, 'Isn't that your brother at the end of the hall?'

He was just sitting on a seat next to the door and I walked down to him asking, 'Is that you? Is that you?'

He was saying 'yes' and I reached out to touch him. I expected him not to be there as I was dreaming, but I physically touched him and then I threw my arms around him and was crying and saying, 'I'm so glad you're back.'

I don't even remember waking up, but the next minute my

outstretched arms caught the mirror that usually sits on the windowsill next to my bed. The cat had knocked it down while I was dreaming, and had I not been sitting up with my arms outstretched to hug my brother it would've landed on my face. I'd hate to think what damage it might have done as it was a big heavy mirror, about a meter round with a large beveled wooden frame.

After the dream, I put the mirror back up on the windowsill. I wasn't freaked out or afraid or anything. I just had this incredible sense of peace about me. I spoke out loud to my brother. 'Wow, thank you.' I truly believe he saved me from being hurt.

I don't have any reason or logical explanation for this dream and for me catching the mirror, but I know it happened and it's as real as me sitting here talking to you now.

Paul Hawker, *Secret Affairs of the Soul*

Goodbye for now

Waving goodbye seemed the natural thing for Benjamin's mother to do.

The day of my mother's funeral, my wife, Mollie, and I visited my cousin and her husband at Mother's house. We stayed well into the night, and then Mollie and I got into the car. I put the key in the ignition, and, as I did I looked up. About ten yards away, I saw my mother standing in the doorway behind the clear glass storm door! She would always stand in the doorway out of kindness and courtesy to make sure we had gotten safely to the car. This was a common practice of hers – I had seen it a thousand times. The inside door was open so the light from the house was illuminating Mother from the back and the porch light was illuminating her from the front. She appeared to be in good health and was very solid. She was there waving good-bye. She seemed relieved – less tired, less stressful. I got the definite impression that this was a 'don't worry' type of message.

Instantly, I had a tremendous physical feeling, almost like being pinned to the ground. It was like a wave came over me and went completely through me from head to toe. It seemed like an eternity yet it seemed like a split second. I tried to speak but I couldn't. At the same time, Mollie said, 'Ben, I just saw your mother in the doorway!' I bowed my head and said, 'So did I,' and I began to cry. That was the first time I had shed any tears over my mother's death. I have never wept so hard in my entire life. And I felt a sense of relief, like 'good-bye for now'.

Kenneth Ring and Evelyn Elsaesser Valarino,
Lessons from the Light

Saying goodbye

The writer Frederick Buechner describes an unusual farewell.

On 5th March 1986 a very good friend of mine died. He was an Englishman – a witty, elegant, many-faceted man. One morning in his sixty-eighth year he simply didn't wake up. Which was about as easy a way as he could possibly have done it. But it wasn't easy for the people he left behind because it gave us no chance to say good-bye, either in words, if we turned out to be up to that, or in some unspoken way if we weren't. A couple of months later my wife and I were staying with his widow overnight in Charleston, South Carolina, when I had a short dream about him.

I dreamed that he was standing there in the dark guest room, where my wife and I were asleep, looking very much the way he always did in the navy blue jersey and white slacks that he often wore, and I told him how much we missed him and how glad I was to see him again, and so on. He acknowledged that somehow. Then I said, 'Are you really there, Dudley?' I meant was he there in fact and truth, or was I merely dreaming that he was? His answer was that he was really there. And then I said, 'Can you prove it?' 'Of course,' he said. Then he plucked a strand of blue wool out of his jersey and tossed it to me, and I caught it between my index finger and my thumb, and the feel of it was so palpable and so real that it woke me up. That's all there was to the dream. But it was as if he had come on purpose to do what he had done and then left. When I told that dream at breakfast the next morning, I had hardly finished when my wife spoke. She said she had noticed the strand of wool on the carpet when she was getting dressed. She was sure it hadn't been there the night before. I thought I was losing my mind, and I rushed upstairs to see, and there it was – a little tangle of navy blue wool that I have in my wallet today.

Frederick Buechner, *The Clown in the Belfry*

Life after death

Awe and comfort are strongly conveyed in this experience.

My mother passed away in May 1921. One night, about 1.30 a.m., I got out of bed and went to the bathroom. I will admit I had been sound asleep and was probably sleepy when I sat down in the bathroom with my head in my hands as you will please now try to visualize. I sat there looking at the floor, thinking of various things, when suddenly I became acutely conscious of someone or something in the hallway. The bathroom door was open, and I was gripped with great fear as a bright golden light appeared on the bathroom floor, and I feared to turn my head to look. I finally did, and there before me stood my mother. It is not possible for me to describe what I saw, but I know now from the expression in her eyes, that she wanted me to know there is life after death.

Timothy Beardsworth, *A Sense of Presence*

Forgiven

This woman received a message which was particularly important to her.

My husband died 19 years ago when I was 58 years old. I was tearful, still I suppose in a state of shock, and haunted by incidents, in the near past particularly, when I could have been more sensitive to his needs, more understanding, in fact more loving. The service of Matins proceeded until we came to the Collect for the day (21st after Trinity) in which we prayed for pardon and peace, for cleansing and a quiet mind. The familiar words came to me with great impact as exactly meeting my needs, and as I accepted God's forgiveness, I was aware of my husband's presence with me and he was saying, 'And I forgive you too, and there are things for which I need your forgiveness,' and then he said, 'Live close to God and I shall be near you.'

I can't describe the vividness of this experience. I saw nothing, and nothing was audible, and yet all this was conveyed to me.

Timothy Beardsworth, *A Sense of Presence*

A mother's love

Jo will never forget what she saw as a nurse on night duty.

I was a junior probationer, aged 18 or 19, at Bristol General Hospital. The top ward was a midwifery ward and I was told to go up at four-hourly intervals to tend a young woman who was desperately ill. I had to swab her three times during the night - at 10 o'clock, two in the morning and again at six a.m.

She had had a forceps delivery and infection had set in, she had puerperal fever. In those days we didn't have antibiotics, we had to fight the infection with disinfectant swabs. She was too ill to see her baby, who was born safe and well.

It was two in the morning and I had finished swabbing her. Her temperature was dangerously high. I went outside the ward to empty the bedpan and wash my hands. In those days we had to come back to the ward to wash our hands again, which I did, at the sink which was opposite her bed. I turned round, and saw a woman with long black plaits bending over the patient. She was wearing an old-fashioned nightdress with frills around her wrists. I was petrified, I turned away in fright.

When I turned back the apparition had gone. I told some of the other nurses what I had seen and they said I had 'night nurse paralysis': when the ward was very quiet you sometimes felt you couldn't get out of your chair. But that was something else entirely.

In the morning I went up to the ward to swab the patient again. She looked completely different, her temperature was down and she was much more comfortable. I said, 'You have a lovely baby. His grandparents will be proud.' She replied, 'His grandpa will, but my mother died when I was little.' Before I could think I said, 'Did she have long black plaits?' 'How did you know?' asked the young woman. I said something non-committal, like, 'Oh, lots of women wore their hair like that, didn't they?'

In my own mind I believe her mother had come to look after her. My mother also died when I was young. My older sister often told me she saw her at the bottom of the bed. How do you account for these things?

Parting gift

John Tavener believes his neighbour was somehow involved in one of his musical compositions.

A neighbour of mine who lived over the road died very suddenly, and his wife came over and asked me if I would come. And I prayed by his body, and came back, and recollected myself; and very soon after – suddenly, it seemed to come from nowhere – a piece of music was fully born in me. I sat down and wrote it, just like that, and it contained only one word – I don't know why, I hadn't been thinking of it – it was the Greek word for glory: *Doxa*. It lasts around ten minutes but it was a very strange experience because it appeared to have been a gift from this man.

Gerald Priestland, *The Case Against God*

A change of heart

Thomas Merton felt 'reborn' after his first real experience of prayer.

I was in my room. It was night. The light was on. Suddenly it seemed to me that Father, who had now been dead more than a year, was there with me. The sense of his presence was as vivid and as real and as startling as if he had touched my arm or spoken to me. The whole thing passed in a flash, but in that flash, instantly, I was overwhelmed with a sudden and profound insight into the misery and corruption of my own soul, and I was pierced deeply with a light that made me realize something of the condition I was in, and I was filled with horror at what I saw, and my whole being rose up in revolt against what was within me, and my soul desired escape and liberation and freedom from all this with an intensity and an urgency unlike anything I had ever known before. And now I think for the first time in my whole life I really began to pray – praying not with my lips and with my intellect and my imagination, but praying out of the very roots of my life and of my being, and praying to the God I had never known, to reach down towards me out of His darkness and to help me to get free of the thousand terrible things that held my will in their slavery . . .

How do I know it was not merely my own imagination, or something that could be traced to a purely natural, psychological cause – I mean the part about my father? It is impossible to say. I do not offer any explanation. And I have always had a great antipathy for everything that smells of necromancy – table-turning and communications with the dead, and I would never deliberately try to enter in to any such thing. But whether it was imagination or nerves or whatever else it may have been, I can say truly that I did feel, most vividly, as if my father were present there, and the consequences that I have described followed from this, as though he had communicated to me without words an interior light from God, about the condition of my own soul – although I wasn't even sure I had a soul.

Thomas Merton, *The Seven Storey Mountain* (abridged)

Communion of saints

J. B. Phillips describes how he received help from a fellow-writer, C. S. Lewis.

Many of us who believe in what is technically known as the Communion of Saints, must have experienced the sense of nearness, for a fairly short time, of those whom we love soon after they have died. This has certainly happened to me several times. But the late C. S. Lewis, whom I did not know very well, and had only seen in the flesh once, but with whom I had corresponded a fair amount, gave me an unusual experience.

A few days after his death while I was watching television he 'appeared' sitting in a chair within a few feet of me, and spoke a few words which were particularly relevant to the difficult circumstances through which I was passing. He was ruddier in complexion than ever, grinning all over his face and, as the old-fashioned saying has it, positively glowing with health.

The interesting thing to me was that I had not been thinking about him at all. I was neither alarmed nor surprised nor did I look up to see the hole in the ceiling that he made on his arrival. He was just there, 'large as life and twice as natural'!

A week later, this time when I was in bed reading before going to sleep, he appeared again, even more rosily radiant than before, and repeated to me the same message, one that was very important to me at the time.

I was a little puzzled by this, and I mentioned it to a certain saintly Bishop who was then living in retirement here in Dorset. His reply was, 'My dear John, this sort of thing is happening all the time.'

J. B. Phillips and Denis Duncan (eds),
Through the Year with J. B. Phillips

Spiritual guide

This brief account leaves many questions unanswered.

Suddenly it happened. It was not a vision. After all, a vision is only sight. The spirit (I hate to use the word as it is not correct, but I cannot find a better) of St Thérèse of Lisieux was in my presence, not as someone I had just met, but as someone I had always known.

My guest was with me night and day from October until the following June, in constant spiritual and intellectual communion. Naturally, St Thérèse wished me to draw nearer to God, and this union, almost hypostatic, was achieved. I seemed to be participating in the very nature of God.

On another level, and in complete control, I lived my daily life more efficiently, more conscientiously and more affectionately.

Basil Douglas Smith, *The Mystics Come to Harley Street*

Transfigured

Six days later, Jesus took with him Peter and James and his brother John and led them up a high mountain, by themselves. And he was transfigured before them, and his face shone like the sun, and his clothes became dazzling white. Suddenly there appeared to them Moses and Elijah, talking with him. Then Peter said to Jesus, 'Lord, it is good for us to be here; if you wish, I will make three dwellings here, one for you, one for Moses, and one for Elijah.' While he was still speaking, suddenly a bright cloud overshadowed them, and from the cloud a voice said, 'This is my Son, the Beloved; with him I am well pleased; listen to him!' When the disciples heard this, they fell to the ground and were overcome by fear. But Jesus came and touched them, saying, 'Get up and do not be afraid.' And when they looked up, they saw no one except Jesus himself alone.

Matthew 17.1–8

5

Unmistakably – Jesus!

Meeting Jesus now

How do you react when someone tells you they met Jesus, that he was there in the room with them? Dismiss them as 'cranky' and view them with reserve? Or envy them their certainty and wish it would happen to you?

The New Testament describes a number of appearances of Jesus after his death. On the first Easter Day he appeared to the disciples, changing their fear and confusion into peace. For some reason Thomas wasn't with the others when it happened. He refuses to accept the testimony of his friends, declaring: 'Unless I see the mark of the nails in his hands, and put my finger in the mark of the nails and my hand in his side, I will not believe' (John 20.25). How I love Thomas's honesty. He can't be persuaded on the strength of others' conviction, and won't pretend he is. He receives a visitation of his own.

There are plenty of people who believe they've met Jesus today. To some he has appeared in dreams and visions – we explore those in Chapter 8. To others he appears in everyday life – as they sit in a room, or walk along a road. Does Jesus come as a reward for good behaviour or to the spiritually deserving? Not if these stories are to be taken at face value. Rather, he seems to have a special care for people in prison, for the sick and others at the end of their own resources.

In this chapter you can also read of Jesus appearing to searchers after faith, including a Sikh boy, a Jewish teenager and a Muslim woman. Notice how Jesus never rebukes or criticizes.

The only good person who has ever lived comes not to advise or improve us, but offering support, warmth, humour and self-acceptance.

Touch me and see; for a ghost does not have flesh and bones as you see that I have.

Luke 24.39

A vivid encounter

A dream, a vision, or a real presence? The feelings conveyed in this story are very strong.

My first experience was at night. I had been lying in bed praying. I was pulled away from praying by a light in the hallway outside my room. The light seemed to be coming from down the hall, outside my view. As I watched, the light grew brighter. It seemed to be coming down the hall toward my room.

Then I saw Jesus carrying a candelabra with seven lit candles. He was tall and dressed in a dark blue/purple robe that had crescent moons and stars on it. The edge of the garment and sleeves were trimmed in gold.

He walked into my room, placed the candelabra on the floor, and knelt to pray by the side of my bed.

I moved my right hand and touched his hair.

I shall never forget the way his hair felt. I was engulfed with his love and the soft glow he and the candles brought into the room.

After a while, he picked up the candelabra and walked toward the door. As he walked out of the doorway, I asked, 'How can I reach you again?'

He turned and smiled. A warm, radiant smile that had an amused turn to it. His eyes danced playfully, lovingly.

'I'm in the phone book,' he replied.

He turned and walked away while I found myself wondering how he would be listed in the phone book. How would I find him? And then I knew that he would be listed under 'Emmanuel'. When I looked up Emmanuel in the dictionary the next day, I discovered that Emmanuel means 'God is present in the world.'

G. Scott Sparrow, *I Am With You Always*

Tattoo on my spirit

Andy met Jesus when he was on remand after many crimes. He is now in Christian ministry.

Sitting huddled in my cell I thought about suicide. I couldn't see my wife or baby son and I was locked up 24 hours a day except for mealtimes. A prison officer used to look in on me. He said, 'Do you want to see the prison chaplain?' I said yes, just so I could speak to someone. I'd never been to church or read a Bible, I knew nothing about religion.

The next day the chaplain came in. He seemed like a nice man, he asked what I was in for, did I have a family. He said a short prayer and left a Gideon New Testament. I didn't think anything of it – when he'd gone I tore a page of plain paper out of it to make a roll-up.

There was a pipe in the room which led to the next cell, the man next door and I could have conversations through it. That night he said, 'Do you believe in God?' I said, 'There must be something there.' I don't know why I picked up the Bible but I did and read the first two chapters of Matthew, which tell how Jesus was born. When the prison officer shouted 'Lights out' I felt something stir inside me. I wanted to carry on reading. I said, 'God, don't let the lights go out.' But they did.

Within minutes there was someone else in the cell. I knew it was Jesus. He told me the rest of the gospel story, how he healed the sick, how he had to die on the cross. Then he showed me everything I had done. I saw it all as if I was watching myself on TV, not just burglaries but worse, gross things I couldn't mention here. Yet all the time I was seeing it I never felt condemned. I said, 'Were you there when I did that?' He said, 'Yes, I saw you do that. I've forgiven you.' I said, 'Lord, I'm sorry.' I knew I was forgiven.

Morning came and the first thing I wanted to do was read the Bible. I started at Matthew 2 but before I read I knew what was going to happen – Jesus had told me. When the cell door opened for showers and I went out I knew I was born again. Normally all I saw was the grey corridor with doors slamming, a grim and awful sight. This morning I saw it with different eyes. I looked at people I'd hated and felt love for them. I had the peace that passes understanding, though I didn't know the phrase at the time.

I got washed and shaved and had breakfast then went back to my cell. God's presence was there and I knew I was loved by God completely. Just like the tattoos on my body which won't go away, the whole thing is like a tattoo on my spirit. I can't ever forget it.

A walk on the beach

After falling from grace as a government minister, Jonathan Aitken took a long and painful journey of self-discovery. He describes a turning point.

It happened on an early autumn walk along the beach at Sandwich bay . . . There was not a cloud in the sky or a breath of wind on the sea . . . The beach was totally deserted and I was a good two miles from the nearest house, so I was able to drink in this beautiful moment of maritime solitude with deep contentment.

Suddenly, yet quietly, I became aware of someone else's presence on the beach. For a moment I thought I heard the crunch of footsteps on the shingle behind me, but when I turned round no one was there. But someone was – I sensed them, strongly at first, and then overwhelmingly. Again I looked around, particularly on my right, for the presence felt as though it had drawn alongside me, but all I could see was the sun, whose rays seemed to be blazing even more intensely.

'Slow down', said a gentle voice somewhere inside my head. It was not an audible or even a human voice, but I knew it was speaking to me. So I obeyed and slowed my pace.

The next extraordinary happening was that tears started to trickle down my cheeks for no reason at all except that I was feeling blissfully happy. Once again I felt overwhelmed by the invisible presence that was so close to me – in the sun, perhaps, or beside me, or inside me, but undoubtedly right there with me. And then amidst swelling feelings of joy, that gentle voice spoke again, saying words which were very close to this: 'Slow down. The road ahead of you is longer and harder than you think. But keep on it. Keep praying. Keep trying to find the way. Trust, believe, and you will discover the path. Do not worry about your problems. They will test you but I will guide you. I have work for you to do. I will show you the way. I love you.'

Then I shed a few more happy tears, feeling utterly insignificant yet totally protected and loved as this amazing presence gently faded away and I floated back to reality, wondering what on earth had been going on.

Jonathan Aitken, *Pride and Perjury*

I met him

Roy Trevivian recalls vividly his feelings as a bored and frustrated 15-year-old.

My parents (God bless them) created a home where going to church was quite normal. I loathed it. Church services, and especially the sermons, bored me stiff. I had heard hundreds of sermons and sung hymns on thousands of occasions, and none of it connected with what my life was about. None of it connected with my passion for cricket and football, the cinema or my growing interest in girls. The preachers were in a world of their own. They certainly didn't sound as though they knew anything about the world I lived in.

Until that one night! The preacher wasn't even a 'Reverend'. He was a layman called Eddie Horton. That night he said, 'Jesus loves you'. He must have said lots of other things, but that's the bit I remembered. Jesus loves me? I suddenly felt a tremendous need to know if that was true.

As was our custom as a family, we all went home, each to do their own 'thing'. I sat around for a while, and then without telling any of them what I was doing I walked out of the house, towards the lane that led to a small grassy hill. I went out to look for Jesus. I did. I know it sounds mad, but that is what I was doing. I got to the top of the hill. It was a dark night, no moon. I was alone. 'Where are you, Jesus?' I asked.

He was there. Quite simply there. I knelt down in the grass. It was muddy. What happened then is beyond the power of my words to describe. I knew that he knew me. I knew that he loved me. It wasn't sentimental. I didn't cry with relief. I was aware of a tremendous joy. I felt accepted, liberated, free.

I don't know for how long he was with me. All I know is that he was with me and then he went away. I knew he had been with me because when he went away there was an absence! He hadn't 'gone' in the sense that he ceased to exist. He had only gone in the sense of an actual personal encounter. He was still alive. I knew that he was still there but not in the vivid way he had been as I knelt before him.

Roy Trevivian, *So You're Lonely*

Restored and forgiven

The presence of Jesus was deeply healing in this experience.

About twelve years ago, circumstances seemed to force me into a corner and I made the decision to have an abortion, which devastated me. A couple of days after the abortion, I went to an afternoon movie trying desperately to run away from my thoughts. I ended up leaving abruptly in the middle of the show and going for a drive in the country, crying while simultaneously singing 'In the Garden.' I became aware of a bright light filling the car. It was as if a huge flashlight was shining from above and the beam of bright light was following me down the road. I sensed the presence of Jesus so strongly sitting beside me that I kept looking for him in bodily form. When the light left, I felt calmed, restored and forgiven.

G. Scott Sparrow, I Am With You Always

Come closer

A serious accident held new discoveries for the priest and writer Henri Nouwen as he lay ill in hospital.

Somewhere, deep in me, I sensed that my life was in real danger. And so I let myself enter into a place I had never been before: the portal of death. I wanted to know that place, to 'walk around' it, and make myself ready for a life beyond life. It was the first time in my life that I consciously walked into this seemingly fearful place, the first time I looked forward to what might be a new way of being. I tried to let go of my familiar world, my history, my friends, my plans. I tried not to look back, but ahead. I kept looking at that door that might open to me and show me something beyond what I had ever seen.

What I experienced then was something I had never experienced before: pure and unconditional love. Better still, what I experienced was an intensely personal presence, a presence that pushed all my fears aside and said, 'Come, don't be afraid. I love you.' A very gentle, non-judgemental presence: a presence that simply asked me to trust and trust completely. I hesitate to speak simply about Jesus, because of my concern that the Name of Jesus might not evoke the full divine presence that I experienced. It was not a warm light, a rainbow, or an open door that I *saw*, but a human, yet divine, presence that I *felt*, inviting me to come closer and to let go of all fears. My whole life had been an arduous attempt to follow Jesus as I had come to know him through my parents, friends, and teachers. I had spent countless hours studying the Scriptures, listening to lectures and sermons, and reading spiritual books. Jesus has been very close to me, but also very distant: a friend, but also a stranger; a source of hope, but also of fear, guilt and shame. But now, when I walked around the portal of death, all ambiguity and all uncertainty were gone. He was there, the Lord of my life, saying, 'Come to me, come.'

I knew very concretely that he was there for me, but also that he was embracing the universe. I knew that, indeed, he was the Jesus I had prayed to and spoken about, but also that now he did not ask for prayer or words. All was well. The words that summarize it all are Life and Love. But these words were incarnate in a real presence. Death lost its power and shrank away in the Life and Love that surrounded me in such an intimate way, as if I were walking through a sea whose waves were rolled away. I was being held safe while moving towards the other shore. All jealousies, resentments and angers were being gently moved away, and I was being shown that Love and Life are greater, deeper and stronger than any of the forces I had been worried about.

Henri Nouwen, *Beyond the Mirror*

From panic to peace

This experience also took place in hospital.

The injections were very painful. I dreaded these more than anything. Then the sister came up and patted my hand and told me a blood transfusion was to be set up. I fell into a complete, utter and absolute panic. I should scream and no one screams in hospital – panic mounted. What should I do? I did not think to pray. Then Jesus stood by my ordinary hospital ward bed. It seemed quite natural. He was calm and serene and his whole presence filled me – his calmness and sereneness had a tremendous sense of power and love.

David Hay, *Religious Experience Today*

It's your move!

Catherine Marshall's experience was the start of her healing from a long illness.

In the middle of that night I was awakened. The room was in total darkness. Instantly sensing something alive, electric in the room, I sat bolt upright in bed. Past all credible belief, suddenly, unaccountably, Christ was there, in Person, standing by the right side of my bed. I could see nothing but a deep, velvety blackness around me, but the bedroom was filled with an intensity of power, as if the Dynamo of the universe were there. Every nerve in my body tingled with it, as with a shock of electricity. I knew that Jesus was smiling at me tenderly, lovingly, whimsically, as though a trifle amused at my too-intense seriousness about myself. His attitude seemed to say, 'Relax! There's not a thing wrong here that I can't take care of.'

His personality held an amazing meld I had never before met in any one person: warm-hearted compassion and the light touch, yet unmistakable authority and kingliness. Instantly, my heart wanted to bow before Him in abject adoration.

Would He speak to me? I waited in awe for Him to say something momentous, to give me my marching orders.

'Go,' He said in reply to my unspoken question, 'Go, and tell your mother. That's easy enough, isn't it?'

I faltered, thoughts flicking through my mind. 'Tell her' – *what* exactly? Jesus's words had an enigmatic quality.

Then came the next thought. What will Mother think? It's the middle of the night. She'll think I've suddenly gone crazy.

Jesus said nothing more. He had told me what to do. At that moment I understood as never before the totality of His respect for the free will He has given us and the fact that He will *never* violate it. His attitude said, 'The decision is entirely yours.'

But I also learned at that moment the life-and-death importance of obedience. There was the feeling that my future hung on my decision. So brushing aside any inconsequential thoughts of Mother's reaction, with resolution I told Him, 'I'll do it if it kills me' – and swung my legs over the side of the bed.

Catherine Marshall, *Meeting God at Every Turn*

Get up and come to me

Gulshan Esther had been paralysed since childhood. After seeking healing for many years through her Muslim faith she began praying to Jesus.

Why was there no answer, only this stony silence in the room, that mocked my prayers?

I said his name again, and pleaded my case, in despair. Still there was no answer. Then I cried out, in a fever of pain, 'If you are able to, heal me – otherwise tell me.' I could go no further along this road.

What happened next is something that I find hard to put into words. I know that the whole room filled with light . . . I covered myself with my shawl. I was so frightened.

Then the thought occurred to me that it might be the gardener, who had switched on the light outside to shine on the trees. He did this sometimes to prevent thieves when the mangoes were ripe, or to see to the watering in the cool of the night.

I came out from my shawl to look. But the doors and windows were fast shut, with curtains and shutters drawn. I then became aware of figures in long robes, standing in the midst of the light, some feet from my bed. There were twelve figures in a row and the figure in the middle, the thirteenth, was larger and brighter than the others . . .

Suddenly a voice said, 'Get up. This is the path you have been seeking. I am Jesus Son of Mary, to whom you have been praying, and now I am standing in front of you. You get up and come to me.'

I started to weep. 'Oh Jesus, I'm crippled. I can't get up.'

He said, 'Stand up and come to me. I am Jesus.'

60

When I hesitated he said it a second time. Then as I doubted he said for the third time, 'Stand up.'

And I, Gulshan Fatima, who had been crippled on my bed for nineteen years, felt new strength flowing into my wasted limbs. I put my foot on the ground and stood up. Then I ran a few paces and fell at the feet of the vision. I was bathing in the purest light and it was burning as bright as the sun and the moon together. The light shone into my heart and into my mind and many things became clear to me at that moment.

Jesus put his hand on the top of my head and I saw a hole in his hand from which a ray of light struck down upon my garments, so that the green dress looked white.

He said 'I am Jesus. I am Immanuel. I am the Way, the Truth and the Life. I am alive and I am soon coming. See, from today you are my witness. What you have seen now with your eyes you must take to my people. My people are your people, and you must remain faithful to take that to my people.'

He said, 'Now you have to keep this robe and your body spotless. Wherever you go I will be with you, and from today you must pray like this:

'Our Father, which art in Heaven, hallowed be thy name. Thy kingdom come, thy will be done, on earth as it is in heaven. Give us this day our daily bread and forgive us our trespasses, as we forgive them who trespass against us, and lead us not into temptation but deliver us from evil, for thine is the kingdom and the power and the glory for ever and ever. Amen.'

. . . Jesus said much more. I was so full of joy. It could not be described.

I looked at my arm and leg. There was flesh on them. My hand was not perfect, nevertheless it had strength, and was no longer withered and wasted.

'Why don't You make it all whole?' I asked.

The answer came lovingly:

'I want you to be my witness.'

The figures were going up out of my sight and fading. I wanted Jesus to stay a little longer, and I cried out with sorrow. Then the light went and I found myself alone, standing in the middle of the room, wearing a white garment, and with my eyes heavy from the dazzling light.

Gulshan Esther, *The Torn Veil*

As simple as that

For a Jewish teenager at Rugby School, this encounter was unexpected. Hugh Montefiore later became Bishop of Birmingham.

At the age of 16, sitting in my study one afternoon, and indulging in an adolescent muse, I saw clearly a figure in white (although the figure was and is still clear in my memory, I would doubt if it would have shown up on a photograph). Although I had never even read the New Testament, or attended a Christian service of worship, I knew immediately that the figure was Jesus, and I heard the words 'Follow me'. And that is what I have (not all that successfully) tried to do. Many explanations of such visions of Jesus have been attempted (Wiebe, 1997), but, so far as I am concerned, it was an incursion of the Transcendent into my life. (I am told on good authority that sixty per cent of all Messianic Jews in Israel were never evangelised, but, like me, had a vision or something similar.)

My conversion was as simple and as momentous as that. But it never occurred to me that by doing so I was negating my previous religious experience, and my earlier religious practice. That was as much an authentic part of myself as my Christian experience, and so it has remained. In the morning I was a Jew, and by the evening I was a Christian; not just a Christian but a Jewish Christian.

Hugh Montefiore, *On Being a Jewish Christian*

This wonderful peace

As a 14-year-old Sikh, Sundar Singh set fire to a Gospel to show his rejection of Christianity. He later became a Christian sadhu or holy man, travelling through India sharing his faith.

Though, according to my own ideas at that time, I thought that I had done a good deed in burning the Gospel, yet my unrest of heart increased, and for the two following days I was very miserable. On the third day, when I could bear it no longer, I got up at three in the morning and prayed that if there was a God at all He would reveal himself to me.

My intention was, that if I got no satisfaction, I would place my head upon the railway-line when the five o'clock train passed by and kill myself. If I got no satisfaction in this life, I thought I would get it in the next. I was praying and praying but received no answer; and I prayed for half an hour longer hoping to get peace. At 4.30 a.m. I saw something of which I had no idea at all previously. In the room where I was praying I saw a great light. I thought the place was on fire. I looked round, but could find nothing. Then the thought came to me that this might be an answer God had sent me. Then as I prayed and looked into the light, I saw the form of the Lord Jesus Christ. It had such an appearance of glory and love! If it had been some Hindu incarnation I would have prostrated myself before it. But it was the Lord Jesus Christ, whom I had been insulting a few days before.

I felt that a vision like this could not come out of my own imagination. I heard a voice saying in Hindustani: 'How long will you persecute me? I have come to save you; you were praying to know the right way. Why do you not take it?' So I fell at His feet and got this wonderful Peace which I could not get anywhere else. This was the joy I was wishing to get. This was heaven itself.

When I got up, the vision had all disappeared; but although the vision had disappeared, the peace and joy have remained with me ever since.

C. F. Andrew, *Sadhu Sundar Singh*

A figure in white robes

Sudden insight was given to this writer during a worship service.

At the age of thirty-eight I was in the Chapel of an hotel, when suddenly (during the sermon) I saw a wonderful glowing figure in white robes, standing before the altar with arms outstretched. I took this figure to be Our Lord.

I then suddenly realized that I was out of the body, high up, and could see my body sitting calmly on a seat below.

Basil Douglas Smith, *The Mystics Come to Harley Street*

Journey of discovery

Now on that same day two of them were going to a village called Emmaus, about seven miles from Jerusalem, and talking with each other about all these things that had happened. While they were talking and discussing, Jesus himself came near and went with them, but their eyes were kept from recognizing him.

As they came near the village to which they were going, he walked ahead as if he were going on. But they urged him strongly, saying, 'Stay with us, because it is almost evening and the day is now nearly over.' So he went in to stay with them. When he was at the table with them, he took bread, blessed and broke it, and gave it to them. Then their eyes were opened, and they recognized him; and he vanished from their sight.

Luke 24.13–16, 28–31

6

Can I have a word?

Conversations with God

━━━◦∞∞◦━━━

Does God speak to individuals? If so, how?

The Bible writers clearly believed God spoke. Sometimes dramatically, sometimes in a 'still, small voice' or quiet certainty, through prophetic individuals and through the scriptures and traditions handed down to them. Many people believe God spoke through Jesus in a special way.

Church history contains parallels. God has been thought to speak through signs and wonders, through the rhythms of nature, through church authority, through the Bible and through an inward light, the direct influence of the divine in the human heart. Perhaps there is no limit to the ways God can speak to us?

Many people would claim that God speaks today, but learning how to listen is a journey of a lifetime. The stories which follow concern people hearing words spoken to them, either aloud or internally. Not always attributed to the voice of God. But leaving the strong impression that a conversation had taken place. Touching and changing people at a depth beyond ordinary reach.

> *For God is*
> *a person.*
> *Therefore if I am to know Him*
> *God must speak . . .*
> *Does He?*
> Dick Williams, *Godthoughts*

Dialogue with God

A one-to-one with God healed hidden insecurities for minister Roy Lawrence.

For many years one of my pet hates was the moment at the start of conferences when the leader goes round the room and says to each participant, 'Tell the group who you are and say a little bit about yourself.' I always felt this was a great moment to go to the loo!

When I thought about it, I could see that the embarrassment I felt was a symptom of low self-esteem on my part. It was difficult to deal with because it went back to some of my earliest experiences of life. Mercifully, God decided to take a hand in the situation, though I have to say that I did not much like it when he did. I was kneeling in church at the time, saying my morning prayers, when it seemed that he spoke to me. There was no audible voice or anything like that, just a question forming in my mind. I am not one who can normally claim to have a hot-line to God, but I was quite sure this question came from God and it initiated a sort of dialogue inside my head. I remember exactly how it went.

'Who are you?' asked God.

Fumblingly I answered, 'You know who I am, Lord. You have put me here. I'm the vicar of this parish.'

'No,' said God, 'I didn't ask *what* you are. *Who* are you?'

I blundered on: 'I'm Eira's husband. I'm father to Christopher and Paul.'

'And they are all precious to me,' said God. 'But for this moment I am not asking about them. Who are *you*?'

As the conversation went on, gradually he stripped everything away from me – background, qualifications, achievements:

'Not *what*? *Who*?'

Finally I said, 'I'm Roy.'

There was silence. I felt so empty and insignificant. Then came his word again.

'Yes, you are Roy. Whom I created with infinite care, whom

I love, and for whom I gave my Son, Jesus. And whom I call to be one with me in time and in eternity.'

That was it. The dialogue was over.

God may not always like me any more than I always like myself. But he loves and values me, and I knew then that I had to learn to value myself too.

Roy Lawrence, *Christ With Us*

Three little words

An actress tells how three words had power to change her.

The experience itself was so dramatic – one of the healing points of my life, a real watershed. I had recently converted to Catholicism and was also participating in a training and development course exploring what shapes us as human beings. On this particular morning, I was at Mass. I went up to receive communion and as I stepped forward it was as if these waves of realization dashed themselves against me. These words formed inside me. Actually, 'formed' is the wrong word. They were as clear as if I'd heard them spoken audibly, yet there was no sound. I sort of heard/knew them.

In separate waves I 'heard', 'You are good!' Crash. 'You are loved!' Crash. 'You are heard!' Thump. The image I had was that of these enormously deep, dark, completely unbridgeable crevasses being totally closed up and removed.

It wasn't as if I was a deeply troubled soul. I was happy, successful, and satisfied with life. But occasionally, in certain situations, I felt vulnerable, not good enough, and powerless. A part of me had a residual pocket of brokenness, emptiness, and despair, and it was this area that was utterly removed, gone in an instant. I was left feeling warm, loved, and accepted.

The words, 'good, loved, and heard' may not mean much to someone else, but to me they were especially significant... [*the writer goes on to describe specific childhood circumstances*]. When you're bounced around as a kid, you tend to think that somehow you caused it, that you're rejected and unloved by your family not because they had a marriage break up but because they didn't love you. Even though I was happily married and had kids of my own and my family really loved me I had somehow always doubted it. Also, one of the reasons I had stayed married was to show my parents that I wasn't like them; I wasn't going to make my kids' lives miserable the way they had done to me!

These broken parts of myself had been well concealed by my highly successful career, wonderful marriage, and beautiful children. I'd managed, in spite of my early trauma, to have a wonderful life. However, that grace in Mass was confirmation that I have never been alone in anything. That my God has the power to totally heal and restore me, to complete me in spite of my brokenness.

From this one event things really changed for me. I realized I hadn't really chosen my husband for who he was; I had chosen marriage to prove others wrong. Released from this I saw things in a different light, re-evaluated my marriage, and made a conscious decision to choose him! It was so different from my original reasons for getting married that I wanted to get married again. He was a bit bemused by this, but I insisted. I earnestly wanted him to know that I had chosen him for who he was and this was my way of showing it. We arranged for a priest and one beautiful Saturday morning a few weeks later I stood once again in front of the altar and made my vows to my husband. It was a simple ceremony lasting about half an hour with only my children there as witnesses. Afterwards we went and had pizza.

Looking back on these events I realize how the simplest things can also be the most profound. In my experience, it seems to be the way God works.

Paul Hawker, *Secret Affairs of the Soul*

Turning point

An Anglican priest recalls a turning point in his ministry.

In utter disillusionment with self and church, I came to 'the end of my tether'. In a state of intense inner wretchedness, of such intensity that my mind seemed on the point of breaking, I got up at 4.00 a.m. and began wandering aimlessly in the wooded hillside. This went on for some time until, unexpectedly, the words of the 130th psalm sounded clearly in my mind: 'And plenteous redemption is ever found in Him; and, from all its iniquities, He Israel shall redeem.' With these words a light seemed to envelop me, and there flowed into my desolate heart such a flood of Love and Compassion that I was overwhelmed and overpowered by the weight of it. I was stricken by such wonder and amazement that I burst into tears of joy: it seemed to flow through my whole being with a cleansing and healing virtue. From that moment I knew that Love was the nature of reality. I was fit and well again. The experience is as real today as it was then.

Timothy Beardsworth, *A Sense of Presence*

'Follow me'

An invitation is simply given and received.

I was a solitary person – not from choice – and I suppose I was lonely. But in the mountains I felt security and joy and a one-ness with nature. One day, as I stood on a hill above our village, a clear bright windy day with a breeze rustling the dry heather, it seemed to me that I heard a voice quite distinctly calling me by name. Looking round and seeing no one I felt suddenly fool-ish and laughed rather nervously. Then I heard the voice again – '___ follow me.' That was all . . . no thunder and lightning – simply the wind rustling the heather. I lay down flat on my face and said quite simply, 'Lord, I will follow.' As I said, I saw noth-

ing. But a feeling of awe and a presence passing over me caused
me to be there for some time, afraid to open my eyes.

David Hay, *Religious Experience Today*

'Carry my cross'

Composer John Tavener felt encouraged in the use of his musical gift.

I had a waking dream (I was actually awake) and I heard a voice
in the room and the voice said to me, 'You are Simon of Cyrene
and you will carry my cross.' Now I don't believe that this was
the voice of Christ; but I believe that it was something telling
me, almost encouraging me, to go on.

I suppose I have come to realize what might be the cross that
I have to carry: to bring what I love of Byzantium, of Ortho-
doxy, to England; and although I am not fanatical about ecu-
menism, perhaps I can do more through music than through
endless discussions. I was asked at the beginning of this year to
set the All Night Vigil Service, let's say three hours of music
which has to be prayed to, and I feel that is my cross because I
feel very lonely in this task.

Gerald Priestland, *The Case Against God*

A divine plan

*Politics and prayer are fused in this letter from Stanley Baldwin
(former Prime Minister) to Lord Halifax during the Second
World War.*

23rd July 1940

My dear Edward,
Thank you for your broadcast: it was what many were waiting
for. It ran so closely along the lines my own thoughts have been

travelling that I cannot resist writing to you what otherwise I should have hesitated about saying even to you: at least I should have said it more easily in conversation than in a letter.

With millions of others I had prayed hard at the time of Dunkirk and never did prayer seem to be more speedily answered to the full. And we prayed for France and the next day she surrendered. I thought much, and when I went to bed I lay for a long time vividly awake. And I went over in my mind what had happened, concentrating on the thoughts that you had dwelt on, that prayer to be effective must be in accordance with God's will, and that by far the hardest thing to say from the heart and indeed the last lesson we learn (if we ever do) is to say and mean it, 'Thy will be done.' And I thought what mites we all are and how we can never see God's plan, a plan on such a scale that it *must* be incomprehensible. And suddenly for what must have been a couple of minutes I seemed to see with extraordinary and vivid clarity and to hear someone speaking to me. The words at the time were clear, but the recollection of them had passed when I seemed to come to, as it were, but the sense remained, and the sense was this. 'You cannot see the plan'; then 'Have you not thought there is a purpose in stripping you one by one of all the human props on which you depend, that you are being left alone in the world? You have now one upon whom to lean and I have chosen you as my instrument to work with my will. Why then are you afraid?'

And to prove ourselves worthy of that tremendous task is our job.

Bless you; I rejoice that you are where you are at this time. Don't feel that this needs an answer. I know what your load is.

Yours ever,

S.B.

The Earl of Halifax, *Fulness of Days*

At home in the universe

Vera Brittain writes about her friend Winifred Holtby, who had only months to live.

On one of the coldest mornings of that spring, after she had learned from a London specialist that she might not have more than two years to live, she went for a walk past Clare Leighton's cottage to a farm farther up the hill. She felt tired and dejected; her mind, still vigorously alive in her slow, impaired body, rebelled bitterly against her fate. Why, she wondered, should she, at thirty-three, not yet in the fullness of her developing powers, be singled out for this cruel unforeseen blow? She knew, for the constant demands of her friends had made it clear to her, that her life was infinitely valuable to others. She thought of all the half-dead people who 'put in time', as though time were not the greatest gift in the universe, while she, who could use it so superbly, was soon to be deprived of it for ever; and she felt that her mind could hardly contain the rising anguish of that realisation.

Just then she found herself standing by a trough outside the farmyard; the water in it was frozen and a number of young lambs were struggling beside it vainly trying to drink. She broke the ice for them with her stick, and as she did so she heard a voice within her saying: 'Having nothing, yet possessing all things.' It was so distinct that she looked round, startled, but she was alone with the lambs on the top of the hill. Suddenly, in a flash, the grief, the bitterness, the sense of frustration disappeared; all vanished away, and never came back.

Winifred never told me of this incident ... until June 1935, when she had only three months to live. The moment of 'conversion' on the hill at Monks Risborough, she said with tears in her eyes, was the supreme spiritual experience of her life. She always associated it afterwards with the words of Bernard Bosanquet on Salvation:

'And now we are saved absolutely, we need not say from what, we are at home in the universe, and, in principle and in the main, feeble and timid creatures as we are, there is nothing anywhere within the world or without it that can make us afraid.'

Vera Brittain, Testament of Friendship (abridged)

Infinite love

A walk in the woods sparked insight in the poet W. B. Yeats.

I was crossing a little stream near Inchy Wood and was actually in the middle of a stride from bank to bank, when an emotion never experienced before swept down upon me. I said, 'That is what the devout Christian feels, that is how he surrenders his will to the will of God.' I felt an extreme surprise, for my whole imagination was preoccupied with the pagan mythology of ancient Ireland. I was (in the process of) marking in red ink, upon a large map, every sacred mountain.

The next morning I awoke near dawn, to hear a voice saying, 'The love of God is infinite for every human soul because every human soul is unique, no other can satisfy the same need in God.'

Quoted in Victor Gollancz,
From Darkness to Light

'With you always'

This writer is keen to stress his or her religious independence.

I awoke in the early hours of the morning, wide awake, my brain clear with a peculiar wonderful sensation; the room was alive and someone was speaking. The voice said, 'I am with you always.' It was the voice of God, Creator or whatever you like to call it, and not the imagination of a disordered mind.

I am no Christian or religious fanatic.

Basil Douglas Smith, The Mystics Come to Harley Street

Give it up

The message which Louisa heard helped her to give up smoking, something she had wanted to do for a long time.

When I was about 40 I tried to quit smoking, but the desire was on me, and had me in its power. I cried and prayed and promised God to quit, but could not. I had smoked for 15 years. When I was 54, as I sat by the fire one day smoking, a voice came to me. I did not hear it with my ears, but more as a dream or sort of double think. It said, 'Louisa, lay down smoking.' At once I replied, 'Will you take the desire away?' But it only kept saying: 'Louisa, lay down smoking.'

Then I got up, laid my pipe on the mantel-shelf, and never smoked again or had any desire to. The desire was gone as though I had never known it or touched tobacco. The sight of others smoking and the smell of smoke never gave me the least wish to touch it again.

Quoted in William James,
The Varieties of Religious Experience

Answering the call

Now the boy Samuel was ministering to the LORD under Eli. The word of the LORD was rare in those days; visions were not widespread.

At that time Eli, whose eyesight had begun to grow dim so that he could not see, was lying down in his room; the lamp of God had not yet gone out, and Samuel was lying down in the temple of the LORD, where the ark of God was. Then the LORD called, 'Samuel! Samuel!' and he said, 'Here I am!' and ran to Eli, and said, 'Here I am, for you called me.' But he said, 'I did not call; lie down again.' So he went and lay down. The LORD called again, 'Samuel!' Samuel got up and went to Eli, and said, 'Here I am, for you called me.' But he said, 'I did not call, my son; lie down again.' Now Samuel did not yet know the LORD, and the word of the LORD had not yet been revealed to him. The LORD called Samuel again, a third time. And he got up and went to Eli, and said, 'Here I am, for you called me.' Then Eli perceived that the LORD was calling the boy. Therefore Eli said to Samuel, 'Go, lie down; and if he calls you, you shall say, "Speak, LORD, for your servant is listening."' So Samuel went and lay down in his place.

Now the LORD came and stood there, calling as before, 'Samuel! Samuel!' And Samuel said, 'Speak, for your servant is listening.' Then the LORD said to Samuel, 'See, I am about to do something in Israel that will make both ears of anyone who hears of it tingle.'

1 Samuel 3.1–11

7

Someone who knows me very well

Communication without words

———————

It's said that actions speak louder than words and that two-thirds of our communication is non-verbal. People in close relationships can often 'read' each other's thoughts or moods and communicate without speech. So if divine communication takes place at all, it should not surprise us if it can happen without words.

In the Bible, God often speaks through picture language. When the prophet Jeremiah visits the potter's house and watches the potter at work, he quickly grasps the point that just as the potter can re-use the spoiled clay, so God can remake people and nations after they have gone wrong.

Now, as then, it seems there are no limits to the ways in which God can get through to us. I find it hard to read the stories in this chapter without thinking of the word 'grace'. The grace of God creeping up on people with a gift of love, whether that love is shown in an inward pressure to think differently, as a comforting touch during a funeral or the sweet smell of ointment on the hands of a healer.

> *and it knew her, it loved her it spoke her name*
> *it had always known her*
> *it was amazing it was perfect*
> *it was true, at last.*
>
> David Porter, *The Search*

A higher power

This man's experience held a message of love for him.

It happened about seven years ago. I'd got up early, gone for a run along the beach, worked at my job for a few hours, then sat with accountants and solicitors for the remainder of the day, listening to the stark reality of the state of my affairs. It's safe to say I was stressed at the time. Lost and fearful. Heavily burdened. I felt very much alone.

I had an evening meeting to attend in the club rooms of the sporting oval, but as there was an hour or two before it started I parked the car near the sports grounds and decided to just walk around for a while.

As I strolled past the gates of the oval, I was suddenly overcome by a feeling of well-being – quite a contrast from my feelings moments earlier. The place took on a warmth and a brightness. I was almost at one with myself. I felt as if I had no cares at all in the world (and boy, my life was the opposite to that). It was a moment of absolute bliss. It's hard to describe really. Just a feeling of total support and comfort and well-being. I felt as if someone was with me, and that I was to be looked after.

Eventually, when it came time for the meeting, the first stranger I met, I felt a complete benevolence towards them.

I call my time in the park my 'spiritual awakening'. I now know that there is a higher power – whatever it is, whatever you want to call it – that loves me and is interested in my welfare. It wouldn't surprise me if this higher power could be the same one that's worshipped in the religions – Buddhist, Christian, whatever. I just know what I experienced. It doesn't really worry me all that much what label is put on it.

The only time I can recall feeling this way before, was as a carefree child skipping through the green English meadows of my childhood.

Today I do sometimes ponder over that day in the park, and how it felt, and I do believe I can feel that again. Sometimes I think that is how some people feel most of the time. Was it possible that day that I felt for the first time in my life that I was loved?

Paul Hawker, Secret Affairs of the Soul

In a filthy temper

Being honest with God was the trigger for Shelagh Brown's special experience.

It happened at the time of the Charismatic Movement. I was very fed up because people were saying they had these fantastic experiences of God and being aware of the love of God, being thrown to the ground in prayer meetings by the presence of God. And I was in a filthy temper with God because nothing ever happened to me. And one day I was so angry that I went into my kitchen and banged on the table in a filthy temper and said, 'It's no use to me you hanging on a bloody cross two thousand years ago if I don't know your presence now – utterly useless.' And I raged at God in a terrible temper. And then I stopped. And all I can say is that after that I had the most extraordinary deep sense of peace. And shortly after, when I was praying, it was as if, in my mind, I was being shown lots of truth. I had such an awareness of how things are that, eventually, I had to say: 'I can't stand any more of this – it's mind-blowing.' It was an insight into how things were, and the nature of things, and the nature of God – not caught up into a seventh heaven, it wasn't that, it was a pure mind thing and I couldn't take any more. And so I simply stopped.

Gerald Priestland, The Case Against God

Reacquainted with myself

A spiritual awakening was to change this man's career.

The experience itself is very difficult to describe. It took me completely by surprise. I was about to start shaving at the time, of all things. I felt that my soul was literally physically shifted – for quite a number of seconds, perhaps 15 to 20 – from the dark into the light. I saw my life, suddenly, as forming a pattern and felt that I had, suddenly, become acquainted with myself again after a long absence – that I was, whether I liked it or not, treading a kind of spiritual path, and this fact somehow demanded me to quit academics and enter social work . . . I must stress here that prior to this experience I used never to use the words such as 'soul' or 'salvation' or any such 'religiously coloured' words. But in order to make even the slightest sense of what happened to me I find it imperative to use them.

David Hay, *Religious Experience Today*

A hand on my arm

A widower is strengthened at his wife's funeral.

On the morning of the funeral I felt strangely different, calm and collected, and viewed the whole proceedings in a detached sort of way, as if I was just a spectator at another's funeral, but inwardly I dreaded those last moments at the graveside. The service began, and I held on very well without showing any signs of weakening, then the last prayer of committal and we all stood with closed eyes. Suddenly a hand gripped my left arm just between the elbow and shoulder, very firm and steadying. I immediately thought it was my brother-in-law, my wife's brother, and that he, anticipating my feelings, was giving me support. I remember thinking 'How good of dear William to think of me at this terrible moment.' I was held fast and reassured beyond measure. The prayer over, when we opened our eyes my brother-in-law was standing some ten feet away and no-one else was near touching me. Don't mistake, the grip was firm, almost pressing, not an accidental touch of a passer-by, and it continued until the prayer was over . . . from that day I have felt a different man . . . In touch with the Infinite, the Creator of Everything, just for a minute.

Timothy Beardsworth, *A Sense of Presence*

Stopped in my tracks

Kath also experienced comfort at a time of desolation.

What happened was a special experience that I kept to myself, because I treasured it and because it was difficult to talk about or describe to anyone else. It was a very personal experience that has stayed with me.

It happened some years ago in 1975. This was a significant year for me as my daughter, Helen, died of a painful illness in the March. There was some relief to the pain I felt in going for long walks with my dog, but I was desolate and finding it difficult to go on with my life. Returning down the road back into a valley one day, the bank was high on one side and there was a tree, a conifer I think, on the bank. I suddenly saw that it was alight, or lit up, shining and most beautiful. I looked in awe and wonder at it; and it just stopped me in my tracks, it was so radiant. It was as if I was being shown that there was another reality beyond all that drags us down, something that can be restorative and give renewed energy. I experienced a sense of peace and hope and love and joy.

The experience seemed like a special comfort to help me to begin to move on. It was different from anything else I had experienced, because later I could not recreate it, even though I tried. Many times when I went out for walks I stopped under trees, thinking that if I gazed long enough the experience would come back, but it never did. I thought that if I could be in a heightened state it might recur and one evening there was a particularly beautiful red and golden sunset filling the sky and the words of Marlowe came to me: 'See where Christ's blood streams through the universe.' But it wasn't the same as the tree, though it was beautiful and memorable.

A conflict resolved

Joy felt that God spoke to her about an issue that was troubling her.

A few years ago there was a great upheaval within the Anglican church when women were to be ordained. Several members of our church left when a woman priest arrived and this was very upsetting to me. There were so many conflicting views both for and against, and I felt very unsettled. I prayed that my mind could be 'made up' for me.

In the meantime I went to church as usual and received my bread and wine gratefully. After all, this was what Christ had commanded. I continued praying for some understanding, for God to sort me out. After many months my prayer was answered.

During the communion service as the chalice was raised up, suddenly it was infused with a pinky red glowing through it. It was as if the metal had become translucent and the wine was showing through. Even when it was put back on the altar it continued to glow. I could not quite believe it and could not take my eyes from it. When I went to kneel at the rail I was afraid to look and shut my eyes when sipping my share.

I believe that Christ had clearly made his wishes known to me, that the woman holding the chalice was more than acceptable to Him. After this my peace returned.

The wave that turned the tide

Jill had this experience during a summer spent working by the sea.

On the whole it was a brilliant experience, I enjoyed nearly every minute. But there was one particular day when I reacted badly to something someone said, and it sparked off feelings of sadness and frustration in me. After work I went for a walk and ended up walking down the pier as the light fell, praying silently to God as I went. I let rip all my frustration and anger – what are you doing in my life, Lord? Why am I stuck, not knowing where I'm heading or which direction to take? Why does so much stay the same in my life while other people have so much more interesting lives? I felt very sorry for myself and very perplexed about what didn't seem to be happening in my life.

At the end of the pier I stopped to watch the sea. The tide was out and the sea was totally calm and very still, with no movement at all at the water's edge. As I looked out to sea I thought I saw a long dark line – almost like a submarine about to surface or a sea creature just breaking the surface of the wave. I was intrigued and kept my eyes on it, wondering whether it was an optical illusion. It seemed to stretch as far as I could see to left and right and to be coming slowly closer. I wondered whether this was the wave that turned the tide, and whether if I watched it long enough I would actually see the tide turn, although that seemed like a rather silly idea!

As the line came closer and closer I saw that it was indeed a dip between two waves which was travelling towards the shore and bringing the tide with it. As it hit the struts of the pier it sent waves slamming into the pier and onwards to the beach, starting the turn of the tide. The speed with which the scene changes as the waves roll in, covering everything in their path and moving relentlessly up the beach, fills me with a kind of fear, as it is true that 'time and tide wait for no one'.

This experience made me think of the verse in Isaiah where

God says, 'I work and who can hinder it?' God is God, he acts at the right time and has a time and a purpose for everything. Like the tide, at every moment change is on its way and I can live safely in the present. I walked back down the pier feeling that I had seen a visual message and my desperate feelings had entirely gone.

'Someone who knows me very well'

This writer's experience was the starting point for a relationship with God.

Age twenty-seven I was skiing with students in Scotland. I broke a leg, and students took four hours to carry me back to our huts. During the accident and on the way down the mountain, I had the most vivid awareness of the Presence of God. I was unaware of the passage of time.

Once, I experienced the Peace which passeth all understanding. (Age 31.) My experiences have the characteristic of coming from outside of myself. These slight supernatural experiences contributed to my experience of God as a person, someone I am beginning to get to know, someone who knows me very well.

Basil Douglas Smith, *The Mystics Come to Harley Street*

Perfumed oil

John Cameron Peddie was involved in the Christian healing ministry when he made an unusual discovery.

I was giving a service to a brother minister and my hands were on his brow and face. Suddenly he said to me: 'Peddie, your hands are oily. You are anointing me with oil.' I lifted my hands; we both looked at them. All over them there was a film of oil with solitary globules here and there. It was no illusion; it was a physical reality. I continued to minister to my friend and in a little while he said: 'Peddie, the oil is perfumed.' And so it was. It had a strange sweet pleasant aroma.

As time went on similar experiences of this oil recurred. On one occasion a brother minister asked me to go with him to a hospital to give a service to a young lad who, according to medical opinion, had only some three weeks to live. The boy was a victim of tuberculous peritonitis. After a brief prayer we laid our hands on his head following this up by drawing our hands slowly and lightly over his whole body above the bed-clothes. From the moment that service began the lad felt he was being healed and he was out of hospital in a matter of weeks. Today he is a strong vigorous active young man able for a heavy day's work. And when he speaks of his illness and its cure, he tells of a strange experience he had when we laid hands on him. He declares he was anointed with oil from head to foot.

John Cameron Peddie, *The Forgotten Talent*

Never alone

A certainty was conveyed without words in this experience.

I had an experience seven years ago that changed my whole life. I had lost my husband six months before and my courage at the same time. I felt life would be useless if fear were allowed to govern me. One evening with no preparation, as sudden and dynamic as the Revelation to Saul of Tarsus, I knew that I was in the presence of God and that he would never leave me nor forsake me and that he loved me with a love beyond imagination – no matter what I did.

David Hay, *Religious Experience Today*

A warning bell

Albert Schweitzer's respect for living things was deepened by this childhood experience.

A deep impression was made on me by something which happened during my seventh or eighth year. Henry Brasch and I had with strips of india-rubber made ourselves catapults, with which we could shoot small stones. It was spring and the end of Lent, when one morning Henry said to me, 'Come along, let's go on to the Rebberg and shoot some birds.' This was to me a terrible proposal, but I did not venture to refuse for fear he should laugh at me. We got close to a tree which was still without any leaves, and on which the birds were singing beautifully to greet the morning, without showing the least fear of us. Then stooping like a Red Indian hunter, my companion put a bullet in the leather of his catapult and took aim. In obedience to his nod of command, I did the same, though with terrible twinges of conscience, vowing to myself that I would shoot directly he did. At that very moment the church bells began to ring, mingling their music with the songs of the birds and the sunshine. It was the Warning-bell, which began half an hour before the regular peal-ringing, and for me it was a voice from heaven. I shooed the birds away, so that they flew where they were safe from my companion's catapult, and then I fled home. And ever since then, when the Passiontide bells ring out to the leafless trees and the sunshine, I reflect with a rush of grateful emotion how on that day their music drove deep into my heart the commandment: 'Thou shalt not kill.'

Albert Schweitzer, *Memoir of Childhood and Youth*

In the potter's house

The word that came to Jeremiah from the LORD: 'Come, go down to the potter's house, and there I will let you hear my words.' So I went down to the potter's house, and there he was working at his wheel. The vessel he was making of clay was spoiled in the potter's hand, and he reworked it into another vessel, as seemed good to him.

Then the word of the LORD came to me: Can I not do with you, O house of Israel, just as this potter has done? says the LORD. Just like the clay in the potter's hand, so are you in my hand, O house of Israel.

Jeremiah 18.1–6

8

All in the mind?

Dreams and visions

Most of us are familiar with dreams. While our bodies are asleep, our minds are free to roam, sometimes sending us picture postcards of their travels in the form of dreams. Those dream images may be haunting, exciting, terrifying or just plain bizarre. We wake holding on to fragments which fade as quickly as the dawn, leaving us wondering what they were all about.

Many psychologists believe dreams hold clues to our complex inner lives, and that we do well to learn their language. Others rate dreams as the random firing of brain cells, heavily influenced by what we last ate, read or experienced. The Bible writers felt no awkwardness about attributing significance to dreams. In them God warns, instructs, rebukes, changes people's perceptions and shows them the likely outcomes of their actions. The early church took dreams seriously, and many people believe God speaks through dreams today.

The Bible is also strong on visions: clear, vivid images which come while we are awake but are beyond conscious control. Visions are less common than dreams today, which may make some of us inclined to dismiss them to a file marked 'low priority'. But to those who have had them, they are real and life-changing.

The Bible tells us that 'the secret of the LORD is with them that fear him' (Psalm 25.14, AV). Perhaps God can only whisper secrets to those he trusts with them. Those who, like Mary when told of the events around Jesus's birth, take them seriously and treasure them in their hearts (Luke 2.19). Like all the experiences described in this book, it seems they may happen to the unassuming, the unsuspecting and the unprepared, but less often to the unbelieving.

> *For God speaks in one way,*
> *   and in two, though people do not perceive it.*
> *In a dream, in a vision of the night,*
> *   when deep sleep falls on mortals,*
> *   while they slumber on their beds,*
> *then he opens their ears . . .*
>
> Job 33.14–16

So much love

A dream left a deep impression on this woman.

I once had a dream of Christ, too. It is one of the focal points of my life. It has carried me through many a dark and frightening hour.

He was in New Jerusalem, attending to a group of people, in a balcony-like area. He came to me and did not speak. But with his mind, he told me he loved me, oh, so much. I did not speak either, but felt if he should move on to other people, I would die. I couldn't bear to have so much love taken from me.

I didn't die when he moved on. His love left an indelible mark upon me and I turned to talk with the others.

Christ's beauty and serenity were indescribable.

G. Scott Sparrow, *I Am With You Always*

Greater than poison ivy

This schoolgirl was distraught after developing a rash from a poisonous plant at the start of the summer holidays. Alone in her room she prays, with tears of pain and frustration.

I bent over toward the bed, and I put my head on the mattress, the spread, and I think I must have fallen asleep. It was the strangest thing – I suddenly opened my eyes and I realized I'd had a short dream, it must have been: I was down [at] the Cape, and I was walking, but not near the ocean; maybe near this meadow I know. It was a nice day. The sun was out, but I saw a big cloud, and it began covering the sun, getting right between it and me! I looked down and there was a shadow, my shadow, and then as I was looking toward the ground, I saw poison ivy, lots and lots of it. I was ready to scream and run when I felt this hand on my shoulder, and I whirled around, and there wasn't anyone there, no one, but I heard a voice, I heard Him – I knew it was Him – saying: 'I am the light of the world,' saying my favorite words from the whole Bible. I felt so good, hearing those words. I was even ready to smile at the poison ivy instead of running away from it! That was when I came to. I was there in my bedroom, on my knees, my head on the bedcover. I just kept it there, and let my mind be still. I remembered the whole dream – it must have happened fast, but it seemed like I was there [in that Cape meadow] a good long time! I felt warm inside; I felt at peace with myself. I was waiting for the poison ivy to start up again, but I just didn't care. I smiled at the thought of it; I almost dared it to try getting the better of me. I guess God's words had taught me – for a while! – what's important and what isn't.

Robert Coles, *The Spiritual Life of Children*

Wrapped in the glory of God

John Cameron Peddie was asked to pray for the sick wife of a friend.

The patient was covered with blankets. But I saw her lying in a bath of golden light so indescribable in its beauty and brilliance, I can call it only the glory of God. She lay in that light during the whole half hour I was ministering and I felt God was thus making clear to me the reality of His presence and power. Never since then have I seen a patient so wrapped-up in God's Glory and Power. The Holy Spirit had opened my inner eye to enable me to see the Power at work on that occasion and I believe the same thing happens every time one is ministering in the name and power of Jesus Christ. But, like the two disciples on the road to Emmaus, our eyes are 'holden'.

John Cameron Peddie, *The Forgotten Talent*

Longing for the light

Chris had a powerful dream after a friend's death.

A man in our village had committed suicide. His son David was the same age as my son and my family knew him well. I was struggling with feelings of loss and shock and the terrible sadness of it all.

The week after his death I had a dream which spoke to me very powerfully. I was walking along a corridor with a glass ceiling. Above the ceiling and all around it was a bright light – a source of incredible warmth and security. I wanted to go towards the light, but was unable to because of the glass ceiling. Instead I was walking along the corridor, at the end of which was a rock. At the end of the dream I was clinging desperately to the rock, in a place of desolation and loneliness. It was an image of intense suffering.

In the year since that dream I have suffered a lot and feel very alone in a difficult and demanding situation. The dream prepared me for this. It told me that it is not my time to die but that I have to continue living my life in time. It strengthened me in an amazing way. I no longer believe – I know. My life will go on after death, and it will be good.

A vision of life

Pam's vision bought her peace and assurance after much searching.

Ken (my husband)'s sister had died and I found it hard to come to terms with. Although I was a Christian, and supposedly believed in life after death, I couldn't feel there was any truth in it. I felt that she had gone, and the only way she was still alive was in our memories.

I went to speak with my vicar and told him how I felt. He said I would have to work it out for myself, but he gave me some passages from the Gospels to read, about how Jesus came back after he had died. I read them but it didn't help at all. I kept praying for help to understand it.

One night I was in bed. Ken was asleep and I had a vision. I saw a passageway or tunnel which started in front of my eyes and went into the distance, getting wider and wider and brighter and brighter. A tunnel would normally look smaller as it receded, but this was like 'the path that leads to life' (Proverbs 4.18), that gets brighter and brighter as it opens out ahead.

I felt elated. I couldn't get to sleep for hours, I felt so excited. I wanted to wake Ken and tell him what I had seen. I knew then that we are all on our own journey, a pathway that leads to God.

Out of the impasse

Faced with a practical challenge, Joy received help through a vision.

As an act of faith, many years ago, and during the six weeks of Lent, I designed and cross-stitched four kneelers and presented them to our church as a thanksgiving.

To my surprise, I was then approached by the Vicar and asked if I would design and organize the making of four very large kneelers to go around our square altar. The church was fairly new and we had grey plastic foam-filled altar kneelers.

It took me several years, the first job being to raise funds for the canvas and wool. I opened a special bank account and slowly we got there. I had lots of willing helpers waiting to start. The canvas was measured and cut, and soon folk were working the black sides and longing to start the colours on top. It was already agreed that these should run through the rainbow spectrum and fit in with our stained glass windows. Everyone waited. I sweated and wrestled, knowing that it all depended on ME. I struggled with graph paper and pens, trying to make a running design for the tops. Nothing came. I was in despair. The sides were nearly done!

Then we attended the parish retreat to Glastonbury – a place of quiet and peace, and I took my graph paper with me with hopes of inspiration. During rest periods I concentrated – and got nowhere. The second evening everyone had gone to bed and I wandered into the empty chapel and sat down to pray. I was very cross and upset and prayed, 'God, if you really want me to do this for your glory, you'll have to help me.' I sat in dismay, appalled that I had shouted at God. Then suddenly peace came and with it the vision of a beautiful long kneeler laid out, complete with pattern and colours. Then I knew exactly what I had to do. So very simple after all. I gave tearful and humble thanks. Everything then proceeded and three years later the kneelers were blessed and put into use. All the church members, men and children included, helped with the work and under the lining of the kneelers are laid the prayers of the makers, written on pieces of linen – now out of sight.

Every time I take communion and kneel on the kneelers I feel blessed when I see the pattern that God gave – because without His help, well, probably something very mediocre and indifferent might have been worked. Folk placed their faith in me – but no faith is strong enough without God.

When Jesus came to our church

This dream was so vivid it would often come back to the Baptist pastor, A. J. Gordon, as if it had really happened. It was a turning point in his ministry.

Not that I attach any importance to dreams or ever have done so . . . But the one which I now describe was unlike any other within my remembrance, in that it was so orderly in its movement, so consistent in its parts, and so fitly framed together as a whole . . .

I was in the pulpit before a full congregation, just ready to begin my sermon, when a stranger entered and passed slowly up the left aisle of the church looking first to the one side and then to the other as though silently asking with his eyes that someone would give him a seat. He had proceeded nearly half-way up the aisle when a gentleman stepped out and offered him a place in his pew which was quietly accepted . . . That his face wore a peculiarly serious look, as of one who had known some great sorrow, is clearly impressed on my mind. His bearing too was exceeding humble, his dress poor and plain, and from the beginning to the end of the service he gave the most respectful attention to the preacher. Immediately as I began my sermon my attention became riveted on this hearer. If I would avert my eyes from him for a moment they would instinctively return to him, so that he held my attention rather than I held his till the discourse was ended.

To myself I said constantly, 'Who can that stranger be?' and then I mentally resolved to find out by going to him and making his acquaintance as soon as the service should be over. But after the benediction had been given the departing congregation filed into the aisles and before I could reach him the visitor had left the house. The gentleman with whom he had sat remained behind, however; and approaching him with great eagerness I asked, 'Can you tell me who that stranger was who sat in your pew this morning?' In the most matter-of-course way he replied: 'Why, do you not know that man? It was Jesus of Nazareth.' With a sense of the keenest disappointment I said: 'My dear sir, why did you let him go without introducing me to him? I was so desirous to speak with him.' And with the same nonchalant air the gentleman replied: 'Oh, do not be troubled. He has been here today and no doubt he will come again.'

A. J. Gordon, *How Christ Came to Church*

Wrestling with God

A religious revival swept Britain in the early eighteenth century under the influence of the Wesley brothers. A young soldier, Sampson Staniforth, was one of the many affected.

As soon as I was alone, I kneeled down, and determined not to rise, but to continue crying and wrestling with God, till He had mercy on me. How long I was in that agony I cannot tell; but as I looked up to heaven I saw the clouds open exceeding bright, and I saw Jesus hanging on the cross. At the same moment these words were applied to my heart, 'Thy sins are forgiven thee.' My chains fell off; my heart was free. All guilt was gone, and my soul was filled with unutterable peace. I loved God and all mankind, and the fear of death and hell was vanished away. I was filled with wonder and astonishment. I then closed my eyes; but the impression was still the same. And for about ten weeks, while I was awake, let me be where I would, the same appearance was still before my eyes, and the same impression upon my heart, 'Thy sins are forgiven thee.'

J. Telford (ed.), *Wesley's Veterans*

This whole world is full of God!

This vision of St Angela of Foligno (1248–1309) takes every-thing into its scope.

The eyes of my soul were opened, and I beheld the plenitude of God, wherein I did comprehend the whole world, both here and beyond the sea, and the abyss and ocean and all things. In all these things I beheld naught save the divine power, in a manner assuredly indescribable; so that through excess of marvelling the soul cried with a loud voice, saying, 'This whole world is full of God!' Wherefore I now comprehended how small a thing is the whole world, that is to say both here and beyond the seas, the abyss, the ocean, and all things; and that the power of God exceeds and fills all. Then He said unto me: 'I have shown thee something of My power', and I understood the rest. He then said, 'Behold now My humility'. Then was I given an insight into the deep humility of God towards man. And comprehending that unspeakable power and beholding that deep humility, my soul marvelled greatly, and did esteem itself to be nothing at all.

Quoted in Victor Gollancz,
From Darkness to Light

Left in no doubt

Now as [Saul] was going along and approaching Damascus, suddenly a light from heaven flashed around him. He fell to the ground and heard a voice saying to him, 'Saul, Saul, why do you persecute me?' He asked, 'Who are you, Lord?' The reply came, 'I am Jesus, whom you are persecuting. But get up and enter the city, and you will be told what you are to do.' The men who were travelling with him stood speechless because they heard the voice but saw no one. Saul got up from the ground, and though his eyes were open, he could see nothing; so they led him by the hand and brought him into Damascus. For three days he was without sight, and neither ate nor drank.

Now there was a disciple in Damascus named Ananias. The Lord said to him in a vision, 'Ananias.' He answered, 'Here I am, Lord.' The Lord said to him, 'Get up and go to the street called Straight, and at the house of Judas look for a man of Tarsus named Saul. At this moment he is praying, and he has seen in a vision a man named Ananias come in and lay his hands on him so that he might regain his sight.'

So Ananias went and entered the house. He laid his hands on Saul and said, 'Brother Saul, the Lord Jesus, who appeared to you on your way here, has sent me so that you may regain your sight and be filled with the Holy Spirit.' And immediately something like scales fell from his eyes, and his sight was restored.

Acts 9.3–12, 17–18

9

Rescue!

Help in emergencies

In life or death situations, most people turn to prayer. It's the natural response when other resources fail, whether or not we have a regular everyday belief.

'Before they call I will answer,' wrote the prophet Isaiah (65.24), describing what he felt were some of God's attitudes towards his people. The people of Israel believed God was with them as an ever-present, guiding reality. Jesus was given the name Emmanuel, meaning 'God with us' – an idea that comes through again and again in the stories in this book.

The people whose stories are told in this chapter found that help was there for them in their time of need, whether that was isolation in a Burmese jungle, facing certain death in an icy sea or watching a newborn baby struggling to survive. We're not always told whether or not they prayed. But the help they received made all the difference in the world.

After such an experience, life rarely goes on exactly as before. The experience is recalled years later, perhaps wistfully, perhaps as a catalyst to major change. People use strong language to describe their life and death experiences. Words like 'saved', 'rescued' and 'healed' crop up time and again in these stories. I can only imagine the feelings that go with them. Feeling known, perhaps. Cared about. Loved.

O God, if there is a God, save my soul, if I have a soul!
Ernest Renan (1823–92)

Saved!

The world bit its fingernails for Tony Bullimore when he spent four days in the upside-down hull of his boat after capsizing during a round-the-world yacht race. His rescue took place exactly as he foresaw.

I've only ever prayed once or twice in my life – the first time when Lal almost died. It's not like a normal prayer where you ask for forgiveness and promise to be good. Instead I take a mental journey, concentrating my thoughts and reaching deep inside.

'Come on, Tony, it's time to pray,' the voice says.

– 'I can't, I'm too cold.'

'Yes you can. Now concentrate, focus on the journey.'

– 'I don't remember how to pray.'

'Yes you do. Wash everything else out of your mind. Concentrate on where you want to go. Can you see the alleyway?'

– 'I can't. I'm too tired. I don't have the strength for this.'

'Come on, you pathetic wretch. You're not leaving her alone. Look for the alleyway.'

– 'I can see it! I can just see it, but it's not very clear.'

'What do you see?'

– 'Little walkways, houses with balconies.'

'Just focus on the journey, Tony. Where are you now?'

– 'Turning left and right, going into shade and then light. Something is trying to pull me backwards, I can't see what it is. It won't let me go.'

'Then you fight it! You can do it.'

– 'I . . . can't . . . go . . . on.'

'But you're almost there. Just a little further. What do you see?'

– 'A door. It's big and heavy, made of wooden planks and iron nails.'

'Keep going.'

– 'It's slightly ajar and light is spilling through the gap. I can hear muffled voices coming from inside.'

'Push it open.'

– 'It's too heavy.'

'Push it open!'

I lean against the door with all my strength and slowly it opens. Inside there are people sitting around a large wooden table, talking and eating quietly, and others in small groups, deep in discussion. Eventually my eyes lock on the one I have come to see and I walk slowly in his direction. His hand reaches up and rests on my shoulder and I feel at peace. No words pass between us, but everything has been said. For a few moments we smile gently, and then I very slowly turn away and walk towards the door.

Exhausted, I feel myself drifting in and out of consciousness. I keep telling myself that if I fall asleep I may not wake up. It is now going to take a very special kind of strength to stay alive. I must not give up. I must keep fighting. I must not give up.

My eyes are open, staring into the dark. I have a dream – I can't tell if I'm conscious or not. An Australian warship is coming to rescue me. I can see it churning through the waves, dark against the sky. It's going to lower a small boat over the side and they'll hammer on the hull to see if I'm here. Then I'll swim out and I'll be saved.

Tony Bullimore, *Saved!*

Dancing, full of joy

TV journalist John McCarthy made headlines when he was taken hostage in Beirut in 1986. This happened early in his five-year ordeal.

I was to be in this solitary cell for less than three months, but after the first two or three weeks it felt as if I had slipped into a different time-scale. Days passed without any variation. The food-and-bathroom run and then nothing. I read and re-read everything available. I relived much of my life and made endless plans for the future. But after two months with not the slightest hint that I might be released I got more frightened. So many of my reflections had left me feeling inadequate that I really began to doubt that I could cope alone.

One morning these fears became unbearable. I stood in the cell sinking into despair. I felt that I was literally sinking, being sucked down into a whirlpool. I was on my knees, gasping for air, drowning in hopelessness and helplessness. I thought that I was passing out. I could only think of one thing to say – 'Help me please, oh God, help me.' The next instant I was standing up, surrounded by a warm bright light. I was dancing, full of joy. In the space of a minute, despair had vanished, replaced by boundless optimism.

What had happened? I had never had any great faith, despite a Church of England upbringing. But I felt that I had to give thanks. But to what? Unsure of the nature of the experience, I felt most comfortable acknowledging the Good Spirit which seemed to have rescued me.

It gave me great strength to carry on and, more importantly, a huge renewal of hope – I was going to survive. Throughout my captivity, I would take comfort from this experience, drawing on it whenever optimism and determination flagged. In the euphoria of the next few days I felt completely confident. But soon I found myself wondering how, even with the support of a Good Spirit, I was going to manage alone.

John McCarthy and Jill Morrell, *Some Other Rainbow*

Help for the despairing

The woman who wrote this account had decided to commit suicide.

At that moment I let out a loud challenge into that dark and lonesome night, into that desolation of land and soul and I shouted: IF THERE IS SUCH A THING AS A GOD THEN SHOW YOURSELF TO ME – NOW . . . and at that very instant there was a loud crack, like a rifle shot [coming from the bedroom]. I stumbled through the open door to my bedroom. I fell into the bed shaking and then something forced my eyes upward to the wall above my bedside table and where I had a very small photograph of my father hanging. The picture had gone – I just looked at the empty space but in looking closer I saw the photograph, face down, on the little table and the narrow silver frame was split apart, the glass broken and from behind the cardboard on the back there had slipped out the last letter [my father] had written me. When I picked up that letter and read over and over the words of this beloved caring father of mine, I knew that was HIS help to me, and God answered me directly in the hour of this soul being in anguish.

David Hay, *Religious Experience Today*

Peace beyond measure

After a difficult pregnancy, Edith's first baby was struggling for his life.

My son was a month old but had not yet been allowed home. Born prematurely, he was tiny at birth, and now weighed less than his birth weight. And now, with one lung collapsed and the other on the verge of collapsing, he needed an emergency operation.

The hospital asked our permission to have him baptized – something which only happened when the risks were great. He looked so pale and tiny, quite unable to withstand the trauma of an operation. It was heartbreaking to stand with my husband by the little cot, knowing it could be the last time we would see our newborn son.

That night I spent a long time on my knees imploring God to spare my baby, my thoughts and emotions in turmoil. I didn't see a vision, I didn't hear a voice, but felt what I can only describe as 'the peace that passes understanding' – a wonderful certainty that he was going to survive.

The next morning the hospital said, 'He was wonderful. He didn't need a whiff of oxygen.' Life was far from plain sailing – our son needed special care for many years. But that was 50 years ago and he now has two sons of his own.

A strange red glow

A serious car accident was averted by this strange phenomenon.

The cats-eyes turned red. I couldn't understand. I looked round to see what the reflection was of. I slowed down for interest, wondered what was going on. As I came round the next bend there was a tractor and a cart. The cart was on its side right across the bend. If I'd not slowed down, I'd have hit it.

David Hay, *Exploring Inner Space*

God among the cockroaches

Corrie ten Boom and her sister Betsie were Dutch prisoners at Ravensbruck, a Nazi prison camp, in the Second World War.

Together we entered the terrifying building. At a table were women who took away all our possessions. Everyone had to undress completely and then go to a room where her hair was checked.

I asked a woman who was busy checking the possessions of the new arrivals if I might use the toilet. She pointed to a door and I discovered that the convenience was nothing more than a hole in the shower-room floor. Betsie stayed close beside me all the time. Suddenly I had an inspiration, 'Quick, take off your woollen underwear,' I whispered to her. I rolled it up with mine and laid the bundle in a corner with my little Bible. The spot was alive with cockroaches, but I didn't worry about that. I felt wonderfully relieved and happy. 'The Lord is busy answering our prayers, Betsie,' I whispered. 'We shall not have to make the sacrifice of all our clothes.'

We hurried back to the row of women waiting to be undressed. A little later, after we had had our showers and put on our shirts and shabby dresses, I hid the roll of underwear and my Bible under my dress. It did bulge out obviously through my dress; but I prayed, 'Lord, cause now thine angels to surround me; and let them not be transparent today, for the guards must not see me.' I felt perfectly at ease. Calmly I passed the guards. Everyone was checked, from the front, the sides, the back. Not a bulge escaped the eyes of the guard. The woman just in front of me had hidden a woollen vest under her dress; it was taken from her. They let me pass, for they did not see me. Betsie, right behind me, was searched.

But outside waited another danger. On each side of the door were women who looked everyone over for a second time. They felt over the body of each one who passed. I knew they would not see me, for the angels were still surrounding me. I was not even surprised when they passed me by; but within me rose the jubilant cry, 'O Lord, if Thou dost so answer prayer, I can face even Ravensbruck unafraid.'

Corrie ten Boom, The Hiding Place

Footprint guide

Also in the Second World War, Ian MacHorton was taken prisoner by the Japanese. After escaping, he found himself alone and badly wounded in the Burmese jungle, many miles from his nearest hope of safety.

I collapsed unconscious on a mudbank. When I recovered consciousness it was to find myself completely clear-headed and without any fear. I turned my eyes to the left and came face to face with a pale-green lizard. The lizard rolled one eye to study me critically while the other looked back the other way, apparently seeking the safest line of retreat. The lizard scampered away along the mudbank, stumbling into a depression as it went. But I did not see it disappear, because my eyes left the lizard and were riveted in absolute amazement upon a depression that had caused it to stumble. Slowly I rose to my feet and, with my eyes still fixed upon that depression, I stumbled as fast as I could towards it. When I reached it I went down on my hands and knees and stared at it unbelievingly. There, before me, was the undeniable imprint of a British Army boot.

I traced my finger around its outline, then pushed it into each of the stud marks across the sole. Yes, there were thirteen studs in that boot. Without the faintest shadow of doubt, it was the footprint left by a British Army standard issue ammunition boot. As the joy of my discovery welled up within me I looked up in the direction towards which the toe of the boot was pointing. There, clearly discernible as they stretched away before me, were more boot-prints. They led away from where I knelt diagonally across the wide mudbank. As straight as a ruled line they went, but becoming almost invisible after the first few. I blessed that lizard which had led me to them, and set out to follow the boot-prints.

On and on they led me. Unhesitatingly, and filled with the confidence that at last I was being led back to safety, I followed them. I did not look to left or right, neither did I fear that if I followed this clearly marked track I might step on to treacherous ground that would suck me down to die in the black and stinking mud. In complete and utter faith, I followed the boot-prints onwards, and always they led me across the swamp on ground which bore my weight and took me from one firm mudbank to another. The mud was hardening beneath my feet; before long I was on firm dry earth. I was through the swamp. Those blessed prints made by a British soldier's boots had led me safely through.

The trail continued across the dry earth from where I now stood; on to where the forest towered up again. I had to rest for a short while, for I was very weak, so I slumped down on the earth. Again I examined the nearest boot-mark. The British soldier, whoever he was, could not be very far in advance of me.

The prints were recent. Minute piles of earth stood behind each of the marks made by each one of the regulation thirteen studs. The hot sun had not yet crumbled and broken them down. The man I was following must be very close. I stood up and I called after the British soldier, hoping to attract his attention. I shouted for him. I shouted again. But I called in vain. I sank to the ground again, then leaned back wearily against a tree trunk and took a long drink from my water bottle.

Revived somewhat, I corked the bottle and put it down beside the nearest boot-print. I looked back at the trail that had been my salvation and as I did so my scalp crawled and my heart palpitated with a great fear of the unknown. Behind me, and back into the swamp as far as I could see, were only the prints of my own naked feet. There was absolutely no trace at all of any booted feet!

I got to my feet and slowly walked back along the trail left by my own bare feet. But although I retraced my steps for more than a hundred yards back into the swamp, I could not find even the slightest trace of the booted feet of a British soldier. There was only the imprint of my own naked feet. I turned and stumbled back to where I had left my water bottle. Would I find the boot-marks still where I had seen them before, leading off towards the jungle track? Yes, they were there, those prints I had yet to follow. At regular intervals, firmly pressed into the ground, were the boot-marks, each with its thirteen stud holes.

I made no attempt to solve the mystery, if indeed I could ever have found an explanation for it. Westwards those boot-marks led me. Up hills and down into rocky chaungs; through jungle and out again; across dusty paddy fields. On and on we went, my mysterious footprint guide and I. As I lurched and struggled on, I was conscious that I was talking and singing and shouting – talking garrulously and happily to my companion who left only boot-marks but wasn't there, and whose boot-prints themselves vanished once they were behind me.

Abruptly, at the edge of a stream, the footprints ceased. I was alone. For a few moments I stood there in utter bewilderment.

What did I do now? Before the despair which had begun to mount within me could develop I heard the unmistakable clamour of a large river through the forest just ahead of me. I knew this must be the Yu. The British base of Tamu could not be many days away upstream.

Ian MacHorton with Henry Maule,
Safer than a Known Way

A scientist finds faith

After suffering a near-fatal heart attack Rebecca Beard began her search for spiritual reality.

It was very difficult. Everything I had tried to do seemed to be ending in a blind alley. I cannot say that I prayed for healing. I prayed for deliverance. As I went down on my knees for the first time in my life both figuratively and literally, I asked for contact with the order which I felt was in the universe about me. I needed an immediate awareness of the intelligence responsible for that order. I wanted the comfort and love and a sense of being cherished and cared for. Whether that contact brought life and strength back to my body or whether it took me on into further expression in another life did not seem much to matter at the time.

The illumination that followed was so profound that for hours afterwards I was scarcely aware of my surroundings. I could as easily have been transported to another realm as to have been there in the room which was familiar to me. Everyone had left the house for the day and the night. I was alone and uninterrupted. There was nothing to disturb the long silence and the almost unconscious state in which I struggled toward an unknown source of strength.

At first, as I knelt by my bed and looked at the wall before me I saw a black cross outlined there. It was terribly black; there was no light in it. But as I groped and asked light came into that cross, and it was not light similar to the light of combustion. It was not a flame . . . But it was white with a whiteness I cannot describe for there is no whiteness that I know that is like it. It was luminous and it was alive, but it was not fire nor flame as we see them.

Before morning came, I managed to get up and throw myself on the bed. I was there all the next day. I knew I was healed! Moreover, I knew I had touched something that would give me strength for myself or for others to meet anything that might come to me or to others in the future. I knew that the rest of my days would be given to witnessing to that light and to that power which was able to untangle the threads I had snarled and bring them again into order.

Rebecca Beard, *Everyman's Mission*

A labrador's voice

Doreen's story of canine protection is too delightful to leave out!

My husband went to sea so we had installed a burglar alarm system. At 7.30 a.m. one morning I awoke to hear my back door being tried. Before I could decide to press the panic button, ring the police, or lock myself in the lavatory and call for help, the great booming bark of our labrador, sometime deceased, barked out; the two cats on the bed looked up. We live at the end of the terrace, and have grass around the house, but after a short while I heard a car drive away. My husband also heard Bodger's bark on his return home from sea . . . so our Angelheart, which is what we called him, came to save me from a burglar.

Emma Heathcote-James, *Seeing Angels*

A mysterious caller

Joe will never understand who or what made his telephone ring.

My mother often drinks heavily, especially when she gets depressed. I've always found it hard to cope with, and perhaps not visited her as often as I should have.

One Friday night I felt strongly that I should phone to see if she was all right. I told myself not to be silly and didn't, but I still had this nagging feeling. The next morning I tried to phone but the line was out of order and I couldn't get through. This was nothing unusual, I'd reported it before but been told there was a fault in the area which the company was trying to fix. I'd often thought I should take my spare mobile round so my mum could phone out if she needed to. But I hadn't got round to it.

I was really tired from the night before and found myself dozing off. My friend Bev phoned as she often does on Saturday and we talked for at least an hour. I was on the settee and when we finished I dozed off again. The worry about my mum had receded a bit – in the daytime you tell yourself there isn't a problem. As I was dozing I was woken by my phone ringing, just once. I dialled 1471 to see who had called but the only number registered was Bev's from the call before. That was bizarre, because the phone had definitely rung, but there was apparently no one there. If the phone hadn't woken me I would almost certainly have slept for three or four hours and then gone shopping in the afternoon. As it was, I decided to go to my mum's and take the mobile round.

I went on the bus, which takes about half an hour. I knocked on her door; there was no reply. I tried my key but the safety chain was on so I knew she was in. I carried on knocking and eventually she came to the door. She looked terrible. I sat and berated her for drinking too much and she came out with the usual stuff about how depressed she was. Then I noticed empty tablet cartons, not just one but several, and I realized she had taken an overdose. I called for an ambulance and phoned my sister and we all went to the hospital.

She'd taken three different types of tablet, enough to kill a hippo. She knew what she was doing, she definitely intended to kill herself. I haven't told her about the mystery phone call which saved her life but we keep in touch better now. She's also getting help with some of her difficulties.

Safe from harm

Now after they had left, an angel of the Lord appeared to Joseph in a dream and said, 'Get up, take the child and his mother, and flee to Egypt, and remain there until I tell you; for Herod is about to search for the child, to destroy him.' Then Joseph got up, took the child and his mother by night, and went to Egypt, and remained there until the death of Herod.

When Herod died, an angel of the Lord suddenly appeared in a dream to Joseph in Egypt and said, 'Get up, take the child and his mother, and go to the land of Israel, for those who were seeking the child's life are dead.' Then Joseph got up, took the child and his mother, and went to the land of Israel.

Matthew 2.13–15, 19–21

Bibliography

Awe and wonder experiences

Beardsworth, Timothy, *A Sense of Presence* (Religious Experience Unit 1977)

Hawker, Paul, *Secret Affairs of the Soul* (Northstone Publishing 2000)

Hay, David, *Exploring Inner Space* (Penguin 1982)

Hay, David, *Religious Experience Today* (Continuum/Mowbray 1990)

Hay, David, with Rebecca Nye, *The Spirit of the Child* (Fount 1998)

Priestland, Gerald, *The Case Against God* (Collins 1984)

Smith, Basil Douglas, *The Mystics Come to Harley Street* (Regency Press 1983)

Angels

Eckersley, Glennyce S., *An Angel at my Shoulder* (Rider 1996)

Heathcote-James, Emma, *Seeing Angels* (Blake 2001)

Price, Hope, *Angels: True Stories of How They Touch Our Lives* (Macmillan 1993)

Dreams and visions

Gordon, A. J., *How Christ Came to Church* (Baptist Tract and Book Society 1895)

Sparrow, G. Scott, *I Am With You Always: True Stories of Encounters with Jesus* (Macmillan 1995)

Death and dying

Atwater, P. M. H., *I Died Three Times in 1977* (see author's website: http://www.cinemind.com/atwater)

Cox-Chapman, Mally, *Glimpses of Heaven* (Robert Hale 1996)

Fenwick, Peter, and Elizabeth Fenwick, *The Truth in the Light* (Headline 1995)

Hampe, Johann Christoph, *To Die is Gain* (Darton, Longman & Todd 1979)

Ring, Kenneth, and Sharon Cooper, *Mindsight: Near-Death and Out-of-Body Experiences in the Blind* (William James Centre for Conscious Studies 1999)

Ring, Kenneth, and Evelyn Elsaesser Valarino, *Lessons from the Light* (Insight Books 1998)

Biography

Aitken, Jonathan, *Pride and Perjury* (HarperCollins 2000)

Andrew, C. F., *Sadhu Sundar Singh* (Hodder & Stoughton 1934)

Beard, Rebecca, *Everyman's Mission* (Arthur James 1952)

ten Boom, Corrie, with John and Elizabeth Sherrill, *The Hiding Place* (Hodder & Stoughton 1972)

Brittain, Vera, *Testament of Friendship* (Cedric Chivers 1971)

Buechner, Frederick, *The Clown in the Belfry: Writings on Faith and Fiction* (HarperSanFrancisco 1992)

Bullimore, Tony, *Saved!* (Little, Brown 1997/Warner 1998)

The Earl of Halifax, *Fulness of Days* (Collins 1957)

Esther, Gulshan, with Thelma Sangster, *The Torn Veil* (Marshall Pickering/HarperCollins 1984)

Fox, George (Founder of the Society of Friends), *Journal*.

Goodall, Jane, *Reason for Hope* (Thorsons/HarperCollins 1999)

Jung, C. G., *Memories, Dreams, Reflections* (Collins/Routledge & Kegan Paul 1963)

McCarthy, John, and Jill Morrell, *Some Other Rainbow* (Bantam Press 1993)

MacHorton, Ian, with Henry Maule, *Safer than a Known Way* (Fontana 1975)

Marshall, Catherine, *Meeting God at Every Turn* (Hodder & Stoughton 1981)

Merton, Thomas, *The Seven Storey Mountain* (Sheldon Press 1975)

Montefiore, Hugh, *On Being a Jewish Christian* (Hodder & Stoughton 1998)

Bibliography

Nouwen, Henri J. M., *Beyond the Mirror* (Fount 1990)

Peddie, John Cameron, *The Forgotten Talent* (Arthur James 1985)

Schweitzer, Albert, *Memoir of Childhood and Youth* (Macmillan 1949)

Trevivian, Roy, *So You're Lonely* (Fount Paperbacks 1978)

Trevor, John, *My Quest for God* ('Labour Prophet' Office 1897/Postal Publishing Co 1908)

General

Coles, Robert, *The Spiritual Life of Children* (HarperCollins 1992)

Deere, Jack, *Surprised by the Voice of God* (Kingsway 1996)

Gibran, Kahlil, *The Prophet* (Heinemann 1972)

Gollancz, Victor, *From Darkness to Light* (Gollancz 1956)

Lawrence, Roy, *Christ With Us* (Scripture Union 1997)

Phillips, J. B., and Denis Duncan (eds), *Through the Year with J. B. Phillips: Devotional Reading for Every Day* (Arthur James 1983)

Porter, David, 'The Search', in Colin Duriez (ed.), *Living Poems* (Scripture Union 1974)

Telford, J. (ed.) *Wesley's Veterans: Lives of Early Methodist Ministers told by Themselves*

Weatherhead, Leslie, *The Significance of Silence* (Epworth Press 1945)

Williams, Dick, *Godthoughts* (Falcon Books 1969)

Other recommended reading

Fox, Mark, *Religion, Spirituality and the Near-Death Experience* (Routledge 2003)

James, William, *The Varieties of Religious Experience* (Longmans & Co. 1902)

Mitton, Michael, and Russ Parker, *Requiem Healing, A Christian Understanding of the Dead* (Darton, Longman & Todd 1991)

Wiebe, Phillip H., *Visions of Jesus* (Oxford University Press 1997)